Feminism is Cancer

By Thomas Rogers

For Lena

I.   Introduction

For most of us as children the concept of feminism remained lofty and distant from our everyday lives. We perhaps saw the enigmatic fist-pumping of Mrs. Banks in the Mary Poppins film as she clamored for women's votes, or witnessed the growing prominence of the "girl hero" in mainstream films, all of which by the year 2000 seemed to have determined women are incapable of damsel roles like they occupied in the past. During primary school years we met the classic histories; the suffragettes (less endearing than Mrs. Banks, in reality), those who battled for access to education, abortion, and the right to vote. The history of the Equal Rights Amendment came to the fore as well, and probably the founding matriarchy, figures like Steinem, Sontag, and Greer. Much was well in our hearts and minds.

Until it all changed. The earnest among us who were not earlier immersed struck against the brick wall of Secondary Education, and perhaps more importantly, the internet. What started as a calm acknowledgement moved to solemn rage, and the violent suggestions championed by zealous proponents. It could no longer be seen as a distant dream; instead, a very real and destructive force had taken to flight, threatening the decent and respectable among us. The name of this illustrious ill-bringer? Modern Feminism.

Since that time, and indeed to this day, the originally noble aims of the sister suffragettes have been contorted to pursue every last edge of political narcissism, notwithstanding the destructive effects on society and relationships. Modern feminists have shifted from advocating for their own emancipation to attempting the enslavement of others, in the process destroying the underpinnings that traditionally held Western Civilization together: healthy heterosexual relationships and the family.

Both these elements are a proverbial thorn in the feminist movement's side, nipping and clawing as the herd tries to continue scorching the road ahead. With relationships it is not so much a question of their existence but rather the fact that feminism no longer has any ground to stand upon. Like an independence party after independence has been achieved, it has nothing more to do but sit by snarling at the happiness and joy of successful relationships with a violent ambition. Hence why young girls are encouraged to be sluts by feminists; only by destroying the good in the lives of these women can the bitterness, the feeling of being outcast, and the sexual frustration be somewhat calmed. This phenomenon is quite like the behavior displayed by the counterculture movement of the 1960s. The young people who had not been old enough to participate in the Second World War or the Korean theater had to create a cause for themselves in the place the inadequacy they felt versus their parents and grandparents. As is often the case, the result came in the form of violence, debauchery, and disrespect for those who sacrificed to ensure freedom.

Feminists are much the same way. They have already surpassed the pinnacle in every reasonable category, attaining voting rights, the freedom to own property, and the right to run for public office. Women are overrepresented at universities, and have the legal system squarely behind them, even when they are deliberately lying to courts or seeking to leech off a man's hard work. Females also enjoy a protected status in society, where violence or verbal abuse towards them is punished far more strongly than in the case of a man. It would be fair to say by any metric that women truly are in control, and seem destined to remain so in the future.

Still this is not enough for feminists. More than any time before they demand that girls reject motherhood in favor of draining corporate careers and no strings attached sodomy, preferably with men of poor decency and status. Children remain toxic in their eyes, and the very suggestion that a man should be dominant is seen as scandalous. Worst of all, any woman who does not rightly stick by the Faoist movement is suspect and a target for stern reprimands. The choice feminist means for accomplishing this goal is as follows: surround a happy woman with poisonous friends, encourage abortion as a humanitarian ideal, and portray masculine men as dangerous thugs who deserve rejection.

The outcome? Falling marriage rates, broken families, and a constant call for the government to take the place of the father, either indirectly through welfare programs or by enforcing coercive alimony payments.

In short, even as society has managed to absorb many basic principles, the movement itself is outdated, and thus its purveyors have been forced to find new elixirs to keep their shoddy tent from collapsing into a pile of obese wallflowers. Like a cancerous growth feminism has emerged and adapted, outlasting one form of treatment and another, becoming resilient in the face of murmuring cadgers who do not fully realize the threat that it poses. Just as a cancer will spread and strengthen without attention, feminism has expanded quickly and is in desperate need of addressing. Failure to act will result in more destruction of society, to a degree where recovery is no longer viable. It is thus important that we ask ourselves whether complacency is acceptable, or if the time has come for the true of heart and mind to act and save what is left in our time.

The feminist column will forever be pledged to hatred and trickery; though we cannot win as readily in the minds of those sworn to the gimmicks of mainstream television, if we merely resolve to embrace the truth then nothing can stop us. This is the ultimate challenge: we must be right in heart and intent, to save not only ourselves, but also the brainless fools who march on uninhibited by their belief in the inerrancy of the feminist cause. We must be unwilling to let up, and adamant in our commitment. For every harsh word they toss in our direction we must return with a smile and the gleaming valor of truth.

The blubbery pink cancer of feminism needs immediate removal.

II.   A Bitter Rebirth

Feminism as a movement suffers from the pesky issue of exhaustion. While it once served as the central banner assisting women with their own advancement, it began to lose steam by the late 20th Century because women had little to gain. Colleges already had shifted by this time to co-educational policies, and even in the professional sphere estrogen showed few signs of capitulating to male supremacy. With their newfound freedom women were actually moving away from feminism, rather than towards it.

At the sight of such a crossroad a movement has two options: either mold into a vehicle for the issues still relevant to followers, or quickly be forgotten. The leaders of feminism chose the former path, albeit in a rather nuanced way. In short time they swallowed every irrelevant topic possible, regurgitated the remaining slop, and embarked on a rabid quest to persuade all women (and their bumbling boyfriends) that these slimy servings were like a $500.00 per plate French restaurant. Lines were drawn, and Western Civilization progressed on, staggering from the gas-filled wrath of feminist attackers.

I elected to begin this segment by defining what feminism has become because it is crucial to understanding how the final solution can be deployed. Too often commentators fault feminism for being simply a wrong opinion, rather than the disease it unquestionably is. The entire movement's current iteration is one of constant evolution to adopt obscure, bizarre, and totally deranged ideas in hopes of staying relevant. Feminists know their failure in this regard will lead to rapid extinction, and it has contributed to their increasingly unhinged behavior over recent years.

The aforementioned bundling of insanity has occurred in large part due to the gradual drop-off experienced in the days since emancipation. Now that women have the liberties the suffragettes whined about, most have hung up their white sashes and given themselves wholly to the equities in today's world. There may exist the occasional high-powered CEO or politician, but by and large the womanly creatures have abandoned feminism for a world where they are free to pursue education and job opportunities, while also allowing themselves the possibility of giving birth to children. Liberation and equality, in other words, can coexist with the family and healthy relationships.

Except in the minds of feminists. Starting after the fall of the Equal Rights Amendment feminists began desperately attempting to frame every debate in the men vs. women, pro-woman or misogynist paradigm. One could either accept happily the models now promulgated by the Fem Consortium and media, or risk being labeled as anti-woman. Through this method feminists began to claw back the support they lost, even as their commitment to women withered to extreme and perverted ideas of cultism. Later ramifications birthed in the initial cancer of the ERA have continued with the political gimmicks showcased by feminists in recent years. The most successful of these would be the "War On Women" campaigned championed by the Democrats in the lead-up to the presidential election in 2012. In just four years the American Left went from complaining about poor economic tidings to castigating all men who did not support their candidate and party as being haters of all women. Women themselves acted as willing and useful idiots, lapping up the popular narrative that Mitt Romney and Republicans in general were on a mad crusade to strip them of their birth control, their clothes, and the right to slutification. As much as this image was completely untrue, women went out in the millions under that motivation and rejected the actually milquetoast and quite moderate Romney for the incumbent president. These ladies fell prey to feminist skullduggery without a fraction of a thought, revealing their limited brain power and the danger contained within the feminist column. Only the recent election of Donald Trump in 2016 has done much to reverse the damage done by gullible women falling to the barbs of feminist opinion.

What prevails then is a battered organization willing to employ every last means to keep influence, much like cancers warp and shift to respond when targeted by different treatments. Whether beaten or triumphant in one part of the body, cancer will rapidly shift to the next, continuing in a wild dash to kill or be killed. In the case of feminists, they will pursue the most laughable charges to prop up those sagging, cellulite-packed, chicken leg thighs responsible for holding up the Sour Sisterhood clubhouse. But while Russian folk lore witch Baba Yaga could rely on magic to ensure the chicken legs supporting her den kept in place, feminists are not so luckily endowed. Hence they run around like ripe ducks set for the grill, demanding donations to prevent their inevitable spiral into political irrelevance and asexual lesbianism in the Western World. Thousands upon thousands flow into the feminist coffers each year, almost all as a direct result of the clucking dishonesty and attention scavenging of individual feminist actresses. The objective of this next section, and indeed the entire book, is to point out how feminists adopt shortsighted and self-destructive approaches in order to maintain relevance, turning away any decency they possessed into a massive and throbbing cancerous growth.

III. Mere Stupidity

1. The Sexist Wrath of Air Conditioning

In general, most human beings are reasonable creatures who pride themselves in their ability to go along and get along with others at perhaps a base level of civility, especially in the workplace. We may have different sensibilities but those can be respected in the name of doing the job at hand. Disputes or desires for change are typically resolved through open communication, rather than unhinged hysteria.

Not so for feminists, as we can see with the case of Radhika Sanghani. Ms. Sanghani is a British journalist who published an article in July 2015 entitled "Air conditioning in your office is sexist. True story."[1] Instead of the satirical nature one might expect from such a headline, the author was deadly serious, and the piece itself still stands on *The Telegraph*'s website, dispelling any rumors it is the work of comedians or the mentally ill. Well actually, the latter might be debated by certain people.

The premise of Sanghani's article is that office air conditioning units are set in favor of the male body temperature, which stays several degrees higher on average than female equivalents. Sanghani goes on to say that women who are comfortable in the existing temperatures have the body type of men, a peculiar comment from someone determined to expose the dastardly presence of sexism. One line in key captures the ludicrous, child-like conception of the entire piece: "Welcome to office life, where women battle daily with the air conditioning, and men have no idea there's even a problem. They toil in their dream temperatures, while women are left to shiver."[2] Allow me to translate the

---

[1] Sanghani, R. (2015, July 24). Air conditioning in your office is sexist. True story. *The Telegraph*. Retrieved from http://www.telegraph.co.uk/women/womens-life/11760417/Air-conditioning-in-your-office-is-sexist.-True-story.html
[2] Ibid.

apparent meaning of this message as I wring my uber-masculine male hands in dismay at Sanghani's discovery of our plot: "I have thought of an irrelevant problem to drive wedges between men and women because there is no other way to justify my position as a journalist. If this were really a problem I could easily solve it, but I would rather whine like a spoiled child."

If the air conditioning really was a problem, a logical person (read: a male) would ask maintenance about a solution, talk to management, or perhaps inquire with Ron Swanson about doing something revolutionary like CHANGING THE BLOODY TEMPERATURE. Particularly if other people are cold, which might include men and women, a quick and friendly chat would change everything. But alas, that requires level-headedness and personal responsibility, two things feminists would not recognize if it meant the difference between banging Ryan Reynolds and Wayne Knight. So the culprits are obviously men as a whole, who are somehow colluding wickedly to turn every chick not from the Arctic into a dazzling popsicle to be sexually harassed by Victor Freeze in Human Resources. And women? They are hopelessly lost, trapped as the refrigerator door closes slowly like The Raven's crushing chamber, with no recourse but hammering the Dell keyboard frantically to spit out an SOS letter on the latest version of Microsoft Works.

To be clear, feminists themselves do not want to believe women are powerless victims in every scenario, but it makes for cracking good theater. Calling the proverbial guard attracts legions of white knight males and simpering women who are more than willing to latch onto the overcrowded lorry of oblivion by offering donations, finger-to-chalk Facebook posts, and ended relationships in solidarity with the unattractive and unwanted proponents of feminist doctrine.

Radhika Sanghani is not alone in her sacrificial crusade for the cause. An article released around the same time by Petula Dvorak of the *Washington Post* sounded the alarm with similarly ridiculous fervor in "Frigid offices, freezing women; oblivious men: An air conditioning investigation."[3] Dvorak opens her piece with the following line, reminiscent of a *Choose Your Own Adventure* horror novel from the 1990s: "You can spot them. The frozen ones who come outside at lunch like sun-seeking turtles, cardigans balled up next to them, bare shoulders defrosting in the noon sunlight, no matter how wilting it is outdoors."

Where the hell is the zombie response kit in this office? Again, women are automatic victims, and the article forays into allusions about men controlling air conditioning and enforcing their will on seemingly helpless females. The particularly snark-dripping ending encourages men to change their fashion choices and adapt so women can feel more comfortable with higher temperatures for the thermostat. Yes, no matter how hard these authors try, they always manage to insert their own level of sexism against men, all inside a journalistic article hoping to deal with issues surrounding sexism.

At *Jezebel*, writer Marie Lodi follows up on this ambition of condescending to men by saying they should: "…just wear lighter clothes."[4] How lovely. Or perhaps women could just wear thicker clothes, thought admittedly that might reduce exposure of the lovely feminist cottage cheese rolls that men are expected to go gaga for. But that is alright, because feminists are after all constantly shrieking about women's' fashion choices being means through which they are sexualized. Some will disagree, but it is certainly a lot harder to objectify a hairylicious chick in a niqab than a see through blouse and designer mini.

Much as the opinions of these modern Dickenses might repulse the briefly glancing, they are part and parcel to the broader culture of animosity promoted by feminists

---

[3] Dvorak, P. (2015, July 23). Frigid offices, freezing women, oblivious men: An air-conditioning investigation. *The Washington Post*. Retrieved from http://www.highbeam.com/doc/1P2-38549984.html?refid=easy_hf

[4] Lodi, M. (2015, July 23). Is Office Air Conditioning a Sexist Conspiracy? *Jezebel*. Retrieved from http://jezebel.com/is-office-air-conditioning-a-sexist-conspiracy-1719883384

against men. Rather than simply being the opposite gender and possible partners in the fight against alleged inequality, men are viewed by feminists as little more than moldy cannon fodder; expendable tools meant for utilization in place of women. These lovely ladies were the first in line, for example, to oppose expansion of the draft in the United States, because they did not want the female sex to be put at risk in wars fought in the name of the national interest. This is fascinating because women have overwhelmingly supported the Democratic Party in American politics throughout history, the political association with by far the worst record of involvement in wars of any in the country, as Bob Dole eloquently explained during the 1976 Vice Presidential debate.[5]

In addition, feminists march lock-stock-and-smoking-pussies behind candidates who support increased spending and higher taxation. They take this approach because men pay more in taxes overall,[6] and are far less likely to take government support or be dependent completely on the state.[7] If men are seen as expendable, then it naturally follows that their paychecks should be viewed as useful means to the ends of women.

We would do well to understand how the cancerous proposals of the feminists are broadcasted through their political figureheads. Most folks know who Hillary Clinton is. What they perhaps do not recall is her statement about war victims. During a 1998 speech as first lady she discussed the widows of fallen soldiers and said: "Women have always been the primary victims of war. Women lose their husbands, their fathers, their sons in combat. Women are often the refugees from conflict and sometimes, more frequently in today's warfare, victims."[8]

---

[5] Antle, W. (2009, December 4). Democrat Wars. *The American Spectator*. Retrieved from https://spectator.org/40441_democrat-wars/

[6] United States, Internal Revenue Service, Statistics of Income Division. (2012). *Data on Salaries and Wages and Business Income, by Gender, Tax Year 2009*. Retrieved from https://www.irs.gov/pub/irs-soi/09in01gender.pdf

[7] Thompson, D. (2012, December 18). 7 Facts About Government Benefits and Who Gets Them. *The Atlantic*.

Beyond the preliminary idiocy of such a statement, the future Secretary of State and two-time failed presidential candidate said something most feminists believe: men are not as relevant as women on a basic moral plane. Taken for application, her words suggest the millions who died in the two world wars are not the primary victims, but rather their wives and female relatives occupy this position.

Another side of this cancerous feminist pie comes in the words of a *Feministing* author, who directed her anger at the plight of a struggling working mother by attacking husbands as "useless hunks of flesh,"[9] and called on women to abandon men because they "earn more money," and can "take care of [the children] better." Such dehumanization of men versus the uplifting of women is poignantly obvious throughout the noxious culture of feminism. It explains why they will gladly label irresponsible fathers as deadbeat dads or useless hunks of flesh, while reserving no such criticisms for women of the same order. Perhaps this is because all feminists, regardless of the subject they are dealing with, insist upon the principle that women are helpless victims in the world, while men supply all the Sam's Club-style portions of oppression.

2. Bloody and or Disgusting

Britain's penchant for producing the most dazzling specimens of feminist consequence is further visible in the antics of Kiran Gandhi, an activist and journalist. In

---

[8] Evon, D. (2015, December 30). Hillary Clinton and the Victims of War. Retrieved from http://www.snopes.com/hillary-clinton-victims-of-war/
[9] Fiano, C. (2009, December 18). Feminist: Husbands and fathers are "useless hunks of flesh" [Web log post]. Retrieved from http://hotair.com/greenroom/archives/2009/12/18/feminist-husbands-and-fathers-are-useless-hunks-of-flesh/

August 2015 Gandhi chose to run the entire length of the London Marathon during her menstrual cycle—and without application of a pad or tampon. In her eyes, this act represented a stand for family and feminism, because the blood running down her legs was meant to be symbolic of the cultural stigma surrounding the female period. As she says in an article on her website:

> I thought, if there's one person society won't fuck with, it's a marathon runner. If there's one way to transcend oppression, it's to run a marathon in whatever way you want. On the marathon course, sexism can be beaten. Where the stigma of a woman's period is irrelevant, and we can re-write the rules as we choose. Where a woman's comfort supersedes that of the observer. I ran with blood dripping down my legs for sisters who don't have access to tampons and sisters who, despite cramping and pain, hide it away and pretend like it doesn't exist. I ran to say, it does exist, and we overcome it every day. The marathon was radical and absurd and bloody in ways I couldn't have imagined until the day of the race.[10]

Tampon drop, right? Of course the ridiculous nature of these words deserves additional scrutiny than they stand to find from the wagging army of feminist supporters. For one, there is no prevailing view in developed or primitive societies that periods do not exist. This is merely a gigantic feminist lie created to generate controversy. The supposed hiding away goes back through centuries of human culture—often influenced by women themselves— that enforced practices to promote public health.

In the interests of the reader's erudition, menstrual (period) blood contains varying levels of blood, cervical mucus, vaginal secretions, and endometrial tissue.[11] While

---

[10] Gandhi, K. (2015, April 26). Sisterhood, blood and boobs at the London Marathon 2015 [Web log post]. Retrieved from https://madamegandhi.blog/2015/04/26/sisterhood-blood-and-boobs-at-the-london-marathon-2015/

[11] Carlson, K. J., Eisenstat, S. A., & Ziporyn, T. D. (2004). *The new Harvard guide to*

I do not seek to be a champion of medicine as an author, none of these substances strike as particularly ideal to have floating around in a small village, house, or shopping mall simply to empower confused women. In fact, modern health guidelines specify extreme caution when handling any form of bodily fluids, be they feces, blood, or vomit. No public health official or doctor in their right mind would condone the littering of such discharges in areas frequented by large amounts of people, especially young children.

With feminists however, the definition must change, because sexism. Our lovely masculine women and their feminine male friends apparently believe it is sensible for one to run on a public marathon route while parachuting raw blood and bodily fluids on the track. It must also be true that children, other runners, or animals that might come into contact with such substances have nothing to fear, because at least they will learn to respect periods more, and by extension, women. Never mind that raw blood and bodily fluids are the primary conduits of the transmission of sexually-transmitted diseases; what remains important is the empowerment of women.

I should add that men could not care less about the existence of periods providing women are respectful and clean in their handling of the matter. As with every other issue, feminists search for a men as the monster when it is fact a simple difference of gender which commands the subject at stake. Men do not have periods like women, unless of course they were raised by lesbians. This is a biological reality. Fighting and biting over the matter when one gender could care less is another instance of the festering cancer that is the feminist agenda. Rather than simply pioneering a more comfortable solution for women dealing with the cycle—and it is worth noting that a man, Dr. Earl Haase, invented the modern Tampon—they cry on about the issue and attempt to blame men for something

---

women's health. Cambridge, MA: Harvard University Press, pg. 381.

entirely within their own control. A valuable movement will strive for solutions, while feminism just enlarges the problem, like cancer.

The bizarre fixation with the female menstrual cycle comes to term at the wonderfully progressive *Huffington Post*. In a May 2016 article entitled "14 Men and Women Get Very, Very Real About Period Sex," a host of presumably empowered couples explain their thoughts on the subject. Self-described feminist interviewee "Scott" discusses his experience using period blood to paint his partner's body while they engaged in sex and describes such intercourse as "Nothing to be afraid of."[12] Another interviewee, "Margot," explains how she reacted with shame and dismay when a partner was sickened by the taste of period blood while giving her oral sex and attempted to wash out his mouth with whiskey. As all modern women like to do, she prefaces this saga by saying she was engaged in an abusive relationship, because perhaps that makes his actions appear somehow worse against the balanced opinion of the average reader. Strangely enough, feminism as an ideology seems to blind people from the fact that consuming raw human blood is not a safe or advisable activity, even if it comes in the candyland-smothered juice box of a perfect, intelligent, empowered, and otherwise flawless feminist lady. Again, ignore the possibility of infection by any number of serious diseases. All the documentation suggesting possible transmission of HIV or Hepatitis B and C ought to be lain aside, because they are the handiwork of anti-woman schemers seeking to disrupt pro-period activism anyway they can.

3.   **Sweet Infections Badassssss**

---

[12] Pearson, C. (2015, May 5). 14 Men and Women Get Very, Very Real About Period Sex [Web log post]. Retrieved from http://www.huffingtonpost.com/entry/14-men-and-women-get-very-very-real-about-period-sex_us_572cb40ee4b016f378957b12

The notable adoration for period blood acceptance and its related risk brings us to yet another leg of the gruesome and repulsive journey: the feminist affair with diseases. Anyone who has enjoyed the company of a feminist knows they are strongly supportive of all women having sex without boundaries or commitment. In the feminist worldview such behavior is meant to strike against the supposed oppression flowing from nefarious minions in the Patriarchy, although direct experience suggests otherwise. The mind-rattled sluts who chase one dick after the other can hardly be considered empowered; they merely use the sisterhood as justification to slut it up without regrets. This explains why a feminist woman will be quick to offer herself sexually to a man, sometimes within minutes of having met him. She will proceed to allow her partner to degrade her body in the filthiest ways possible, but then proceed to run around squealing about objectification of women in the world. Hypocrisy need not apply.

Feminism's dalliance with high-risk sexual behaviors like oral sex with strangers or anal intercourse leads many acolytes to become infected with STDs, generally regarded as undesirable. Not so for Mary and the Dildocats. During the throes of a sweet spring the pink coalition began feeding a hashtag on Twitter, #ShoutYourStatus, meant to empower fellow spinsters young and shriveled to broadcast their pride in having attained positive status for some form of VD. Rules the rest of society believe to be sensible apparently do not meld in feminism's suspended reality. According to Britni, one of the movement's organizers: "We felt like if people could dismantle abortion stigma by sharing their stories, we wanted to try the same tactic for STI+ people. The #ShoutYourStatus hashtag is a place for STI+ people to share their status as a way to humanize something that so many people have, and to not feel ashamed."[13]

---

[13] Bussel, R. (2016, April 16). Right-wing trolls attack #ShoutYourStatus campaign: "American feminists now feel the need to brag about what stds they've caught". *Salon.* Retrieved from http://www.salon.com/2016/04/14/rightwing_trolls_attack_shoutyourstatus_campaign_ame

If only such words were satire. What is especially telling about the matter is how feminists use terminology to justify their own degenerate flaws. While most decent people will acknowledge they made a mistake and express regret, feminists remain incapable of such actions. In point, the shouting campaign was organized by four women who were infected by HIV, and displays their sick moral positioning well. Everyone should "gather round and be proud of who you are," even though the disease is a direct result of poor decision-making. Fellating random strangers at university or engaging in rough, unprotected anal sex with tropical island natives is hardly "empowering," but in order to find peace of heart in the aftermath the feminist police need support groups made up of the general public. More broadly, it would appear the goal of the hashtag is to persuade future sexual partners that having sex with these overweight and diseased cro-morons is perfectly desirable. Otherwise any sensible person will turn and sprint at the sound of such infections, but God forbid a feminist is prevented from fulfilling her three second orgasm by engaging in whore-like proclivities with anonymous transmen.

The cancerous tumor representing attempts to normalize disease does not stop with Twitter, however. A recent online video by sex writer Ella Dawson adds fuel to the voluminous fire by linking stigma around STIs to "slut-shaming," the practice used by society to keep severely promiscuous women from destroying themselves and their families. Dawson says, quite pompously, that having herpes is the "ultimate douchebag detector."[14] She goes on to note: "If someone rejects you for this, chances are, it wouldn't work out and you're dodging a lot of unhappiness."[15] Yes, the primary judgment should be on the logic of the person rejecting you for being having a filthy sex life, not the feminist

rican_feminists_now_feel_the_need_to_brag_about_what_stds_theyve_caught/
[14] Marusic, K. (2015, September 08). This Twenty-Something Got Herpes, And Now She's On A Mission To Tell Everyone About It. Retrieved from http://www.mtv.com/news/2264301/ella-dawson-herpes-on-a-mission-to-tell-everyone/
[15] Ibid.

growing colonies of anything but babies between her legs. This may be the start of a glorious new age in which we go about publicly-shaming people who do not want to be in relationships with the diseased. Because doing anything else is oppressive towards women who just want to bring another little guy to the sheets party.

There is a great deal of talk in feminist publications about "eliminating the stigma around STDs," yet the point none of these airhead darlings seem to comprehend is that stigmas are developed in groups for a good reason. Herpes is an unpleasant disease to have, and one which is easily transmittable. Wanting to protect oneself from such a disease goes back to a primeval drive for survival, and explains the behavior of people who decline romance and sex on this basis. Just as you wouldn't shake the sheets with a Wandering Spider, no one wants to have intercourse with a person who has a disease.

4.   Big Girls, You Are Beautiful

The unhealthy promotion major proceeds necessarily to the great feminist wanderlust for the hills of Fat Positivity. Originally convened as a means to build the self-esteem of heavier women (this appears to be the running theme), the feminist wing has steadily developed into nothing more than a rancid video for gluttony and poor lifestyle choices. Presently it epitomizes a critical threat to social and physical health for the entire country.

Exhibit A: Whitney Way Thore. Besides sporting an edgy, almost superheroic name, Ms. Thore is 378 pounds and a "body positivity activist." She is also a feminist who has used fame gleaned from a viral YouTube video to speak on the ways that fat acceptance and feminism are related. Besides her blog and associated videos on the internet containing her imposing and enrapturing presence, she has also been the subject of a television program by TLC. In regards to her views on feminism and the fat coalition she said:

> As a woman and a feminist, I wholeheartedly know that how attractive I am to a particular person, or society at large, does not dictate how smart I am, how capable I am, how talented I am, how well I can serve others, or how I happy and fulfilled as a human being I can be. I know that my life and my purpose are so much bigger than being attractive to someone. [16]

Bigger is not a terrible way of putting it, and overall a smashing poem, right? It is worth pointing out that Thore's epic statement carefully avoids reference to any problems caused by being substantially overweight. According to our vile and sexist friends at the National Institutes of Health,[17] here are but a few examples of the problems obese and overweight folks may encounter:

- Heart disease.
- High blood pressure.
- Stroke

---

[16] Hawks, A. (2015, May 16). Whitney Thore explains how feminism and fat positivity are connected [Web log post]. Retrieved from http://starcasm.net/archives/315776
[17] What Are the Health Risks of Overweight and Obesity? (2012, July 13). Retrieved from https://www.nhlbi.nih.gov/health/health-topics/topics/obe/risks

- Type 2 Diabetes

- Abnormal blood fats

- Metabolic Syndrome

- Cancer

- Sleep Apnea

- Obesity Hypoventilation Syndrome

- Reproductive problems

- Gallstones

I certainly don't wish to be a smartass but none of those conditions are exactly desirable, yet the fat-fem alliance actively attempts to ignore them in favor their fantastical conception of oppression based on the size of their midsections. Whitney Thore appears to be in denial, by the way, because in 2016 she was rushed to the hospital after she passed out during an extended dance session. The doctor's opinion reportedly persuaded her that she needs to adopt "healthy habits,"[18] a fairly obvious dig at the shape she is currently in. Most proper-minded people can see why she might face such problems without needing the doctor's opinion. Whenever we see a fat person performing physical activities they are normally moving slow and huffing and puffing the whole way. Many obese people do not even try to exercise because of the strain it puts on their body, and consequently they remain the same, unchanged in their weight. Furthermore, Ms. Thore also suffers from a hormonal problem enhanced by her weight, and is dangerously close to becoming a diabetic.[19] To a strong feminist such facts are threatening, while the rest of the population

---

[18] Mazziotta, J. (2015, June 15). WATCH: Whitney Way Thore Gets a Wake-Up Call at the Hospital – 'I Need to Have Healthy Habits' *People*. Retrieved from http://people.com/bodies/whitney-way-thore-gets-a-wake-up-call-at-the-hospital/
[19] Davies, Madlen. "'I'm 27 stone but have NO desire to be thin': Fat Girl Dancing and TV star Whitney Thore speaks out about her battle with polycystic ovaries – and why the link between obesity and health problems is exaggerated Retrieved from http://www.dailymail.co.uk/health/article-3247597/I-m-27-stone-NO-desire-Fat-Girl-Dancing-TV-star-Whitney-Thore-speaks-battle-polycystic-ovaries-link-obesity-health-

simply sees it for what is: reality beckoning. Being substantially overweight is not some mark of pride; it is the foundation for serious health problems.

The relative girth of the fat positive crowd manages to advance past the handles of Whitney's incredible story. On an episode of the Australian program "Fat Fighters,"[20] various individuals in the fat positive community were brought together to discuss the issues surrounding body image culture and the relative problems associated with such lifestyles. In the segment the fat activists flaunted their predictable claims about empowerment and stigma, while their more skeptical (and much thinner) opponents provided actual facts to support their positions. Perhaps the most poignant moment comes towards the end, when a fat positive specimen is asked if she is healthy. As should be expected, she launches into a tirade of personal outrage at having to discuss her own health, and appeals to people's emotions.

This is by all accounts a solid illustration of the fat positivity mindset in feminism. Health does not matter, and image in unimportant. Any sort of criticism must necessarily be the nasty handiwork of some secretive order hell-bent on oppressing and objectifying women. Of course this is complete nonsense. The only objectification done by those fat skeptics is the general shape of the bodies they are forced to observe versus healthier alternatives. But alas, being the toxic form that it is, feminism can only continue infecting people with perpetual, vicious angst.

I will go ahead and add another telling example of the fat feminism reality by discussing the article "6 Things I Understand About the Fat- Acceptance Movement" by Jes Baker. Ostensibly written as a response to a fat skeptic, it happily marches down the path of

---

problems-exaggerated.html#ixzz4WdlFKiDI ." Daily Mail. N.p., 28 Sept. 2015. Web.
[20] Motion picture on Television Program. (2013). Australia: InsightSBS. Retrieved from https://www.youtube.com/watch?v=v6mMpE8AaA0

endless tomfoolery and reveals the nonsense which a great section of the feminist fat community appears to believe. It is only fair to note that the author in question describes herself as "…pretty damn fat and unabashedly so." Such knowledge will help explain the logic baked into her writing, but before anything else, a hearty congratulations to her for attaining that weight, which is likely more than enough to flatten all the horrible patriarchs in the world. The singular importance of the article sources in its section rebutting health concerns raised by the subject of reply, Carolyn Hall. Baker goes about her mission in a terribly disorganized manager, while also succeeding at torpedoing her argument within the first couple sentences, where she quotes Louise Green of Body Exchange and discusses the latter's experience as a trainer for women of various sizes. Green says: "I have trained women at 200lbs and I have trained women at 400lbs; I am not saying everyone I have trained is 100% healthy, but I am saying my reality consists of big bodies, with big capabilities and limitless lives."[21]

We'll halt the Golden Corral buffet right there. Two things stand out from this statement. First, there is the weak concession that the women in question are not 100 percent healthy. The wording alone suggests Green can only avoid lying by dropping a flimsy and unconvincing disclaimer. Next, the second half of the statement is like a mushy advert for a self-help seminar on persuading your goldfish to make love to a pachyderm. She refers to "my reality," implying it exists separate from what other folks perceive. Here we have another tendency within the fat positivity horde; personal opinions passed off as the sanctified truth simply because they serve a narrow political interest. It would also be nice to have a clearer idea what "big capabilities" and "limitless lives" might look like. The most jaded among us stand otherwise to muse as to what exactly these capabilities can

---

[21] Baker, J. (2014, August 17). 6 Things That I Understand About the Fat-Acceptance Movement. Retrieved from http://everydayfeminism.com/2014/08/i-understand-fat-acceptance-movement/

produce different from others of normal size, apart from the rather obvious addition of methane to the atmosphere, and perhaps cellulite twerking.

In the same section on fat health issues Baker responds to an admittedly humorous complaint from an imagined anonymous internet comment by saying: "Allow me to repeat myself; it's none of your concern. Their body. Their rules." Nope, not quite. The popular feminist claptrap about "My Body, My Choice" rings even duller when the fat epidemic is introduced. Carrying substantial body weight beyond what is medically normal actually has a direct impact on the lives of others, and their pocketbooks. According to studies by the State of Obesity, costs related to obese folks in the areas of disease and healthcare range from $147 billion to $210 billion per year, and the lower productivity of fat employees is estimated to run up a cost to the tune of $506.00 per employee annually.[22] Those last two figures may help explain the complaints in Ms. Baker's piece about fat employees being paid less than their thin counterparts.

As far as transportation is concerned, a study in 2000 showed that fat people caused airlines to burn an additional 350 million gallons of gas each year, and spent around $275 million for this reason.[23] Our resident math whizzes can go ahead and speculate as to how much of those costs sink into the price of tickets, and in America's fat heaven basic flights within the country are far more expensive than many international options. Slightly more shocking to the average goober is the cost brought on by fat drivers. A 2010 report by Allstate suggested the skyrocketing levels of weight in America has led to an increase in fuel consumption of 1 billion gallons each year on average, while the Department of Energy concludes that for each 100 pounds of weight added to a vehicle, its fuel efficiency drops by

[22] The Healthcare Costs of Obesity. (n.d.). Retrieved from
http://stateofobesity.org/healthcare-costs-obesity/
[23] Collins, D. (2004, November 05). U.S.: Fat Fliers Swell Fuel Costs. Retrieved from
http://www.cbsnews.com/news/us-fat-fliers-swell-fuel-costs/

two percent.[24] That is not exactly golden news for the environment, unless one is referring to the yellowy shimmer of oil in the riverbed.

So we know fat people contribute to higher costs because of their medical conditions, which are inevitably borne by the healthier people, particularly through public and private healthcare subsidies. It is also clear the overweight cause us to burn more fuel, a negative in the age of perpetually greedy oilmen seeking to gouge prices at the expense of the consumer. And finally, none of these factors are conducive to the vitality and sustainability of the environment, and nor is the copious amount of methane fatties manufacture due to their "foodie" lifestyle. In short, the entire feminist "argument" when it comes to fat positivity consists of ignoring reality and contradictory evidence in favor the odious and rotten "You go gurl" mentality that has infected women like a cancerous poison over recent years

One must halt at this point to feather the critical question: why are fat-feminist activists so concerned with trying to persuade people of their own lifestyle choice? The immediate answer they give concerning self-esteem boosts should not matter when we consider how feminists refuse to conform to social conceptions of beauty which must invariably be rooted in the Patriarchy. If it is true as Miss Baker suggests that the entire matter is up to them ala "Their body. Their Rules," then why are we targeted with endless throes of pro-fat propaganda? I am willing to offer a solution to this query: feminists have an unquenched desire for attention and validation—from men. The Sulphur Sisters will never concede this, but the relentless fanaticism of their actions and screeds pushes the pendulum in a completely different direction.

---

[24] Fairchild, C. (2012, October 09). Gas Mileage, Costs Affected By Driver's Weight. Retrieved from http://www.huffingtonpost.com/2012/10/09/gas-mileage-costs-affected-by-drivers-weight_n_1951174.html

To begin, no matter how much they postulate otherwise, feminists are not content to appropriate help and satisfaction from women alone. As odd as it might seem, the female psyche is haplessly roped to a basic natural instinct to seek the company and sexual validation only men can provide. A woman may be patted on the back by phalanxes of fellow girlies, fat and thin in their shapes and brain sizes, yet none of this comes close to the satisfaction which a man gives them through his recognition and attention. One thousand women can compliment a fellow female and she will be at best cheery; the same pick-me-up from a man will tickle her like watermelon marmalade. The key difference is in the male's ability to confirm her physical and aesthetic worth on the social and evolutionary planes. In the strictly competitive fields of human carnal psychology, a woman knows her biological clock begins ticking as soon as she reaches puberty, or, for the sake of the American legal system, eighteen years old. Failure to secure a man for partnership in life increases the likelihood she will not marry and spend her existence both without children or the juicy comfort that a male's paycheck can deliver. She may well giggle and reply with a meaningless "You're beautiful too," against the praise of a Best Friend Forever, but this sort of recognition is cheap to her eyes. The lone male compliment signals she is attractive, potentially desirable, and less likely to spend her thirties desperately trying to persuade some miserable illegal immigrant that matrimony and intercourse with her is far preferable to lacking a Green Card when ICE knocks down the door.

In case it is still unclear, the feminists promote fat positivity garbage because THEY are afraid of male rejection and the long-term pitfalls surrounding an inability to tether close a strapping young fellow who is fit (because God forbid fat women should have to do the midnight tango with three walruses tucked into one skin; that would be three walruses too many). These ladies have already experienced continuous rejection by men they found appealing, and instead of trying to improve their state by dieting or working out they resort to brainwashing weak, mostly politically liberal men into the Way of the Rolls.

Beyond moderate Republican males who harbor a fetish to tumble around on top (or

beneath) the loving flab of an elephant, I doubt they will find much success.

5. Feminist Boostification

We can see the feminist self-help dynamic in action on a large scale by pointing

to a video project released by BuzzFeed Yellow on YouTube in December 2016. The goal

of the piece, titled "Women Re-Create The Victoria Secret Fashion Show," is to empower

women of different sizes to feel confidence about their looks. It opens with the prototypical

jump edit interviews of participants—many of whom are employees of BuzzFeed—talking

about their experiences with body imagery and bucking themselves up. Interestingly,

BuzzFeed did not bother recruiting random people from the street, and in fact ended up selecting a handful of women with healthy bodies who would not struggle to find male dates if they were dressed like militant lesbians from Amazonia. The video proceeds with multiple rotund oompa-loompas waddling out, occasionally interspersed with fitter women and a lone, but apparently heavily-modified, transgender lady. A particularly noticeable part of the video features one of the participants saying: "I am a very sexy and powerful person."[25] Such a claim about oneself is ludicrous, no matter who it stems from, but certainly when the source is an awkward model in a contest meant to emulate professional supermodels. After all, most men accept their girlfriends are not going to look exactly like a Victoria's Secret Angel. The Fat Feministas want women to believe otherwise, but every man can see the difference between his own chick and Adriana Lima; it is called reality. Were the BuzzFeed activists trying to help women, they might attempt an explanation of the gap between reality and professional modeling, which exists for a reason. Fantasy is there because we as humans find it enticing, not because it is meant to replace everything we know.

The sad truth is that the audience depicted in the BuzzFeed video is overwhelmingly female, with the choice male employees possibly threatened if they elected to not attend. When the women stride out in bumbling fashion the failure of their effort becomes brazenly clear: only similar-minded women and co-workers cared enough to attend. It's obvious why men would not wish to observe overweight or transsexual people play-acting as models, but perhaps more telling is the lacking turnout by normal women unbridled by the nattering teeth in feminist's sharpest array. I arrogantly submit this is because women—particularly fit women, are just as repulsed by the sight of fat rolls doing sexy time on the runway. Where does this cavernous divide between the normal and the feminists come from? Let us open some further examples to see.

---

[25] Women Re-Create The Victoria Secret Fashion Show. (2016, December 08). Retrieved from https://www.youtube.com/watch?v=45V61KHcr2E

6.   Public Degeneracy

Another prime example of the feminist self-immolation campaign lies with the actions of groups such as Femen. Originally formed in 2008 to combat imaginary injustices plaguing the female population in Ukraine, it quickly morphed into a morbidly corrupt organ to advance feminist social prostitution. Protests pioneered by the organization typically present a frightful leftist message complimented by topless, semi-A cup activists. In 2014, members of Femen launched a scene in front of the Vatican which involved them inserting crucifixes into their rectal cavities while screaming that religion should be "kept inside."[26] The move predictably attracted attention from the police, who arrested them, yet not before the women could keep up their grotesque display for several minutes. A similar video stunt involved an actress with the associated Pussy Riot group having sex with a dead chicken,[27] no doubt a strong signal of their message promoting female dignity and respect.

Both these occurrences must be mentioned because they accentuate the extremes to which modern feminists have gone in divorcing themselves utterly from the demands of reality, while also lacking any measure of self-perception. They likely believe such scenes of self-flagellation are somehow communicating a positive message to women, when in fact girls are repulsed by the surrender to debauchery displayed. Feminists thus appear to be embarked on a suicide run where all hope rests on their ability to continuously alienate everyone who might be decent pickings for a future feminist activist.

7.   Believe as I do

Any lone force isolated from the needed life resources to thrive will ultimately sputter and die. A biological and social machine can only do so much when it lacks the fuel of human capital, and thus is compelled to rely on the cautious drip of societal stragglers for survival. Evolution, in all its glorious forms, marches on.

Feminism in its own parasitical way is exactly like this. The radicalized and searing tactics of the past and present turned countless women off to the no shame 24/7 worldview, until the momentum shifted to its modern form; an angry rump state bitter because the various members are not getting enough attention for their own rumps. Chips-

---

[26] George, K. (2014, November 19). Femen Protestors Shove Crucifixes Up Their Bums In Vatican Square — VIDEO [Web log post]. Retrieved from https://www.bustle.com/articles/49905-femen-protestors-shove-crucifixes-up-their-bums-in-vatican-square-video

[27] Russian punks "Pussy Riot" and chicken in the vagina! . (2012, July 23). Retrieved from http://www.liveleak.com/view?i=aea_1343072683

gorging, Doritos-with-Tiramisu feminism is weakening, and in some ways threatens to die off completely, as mentioned in the introduction. Since they have already succeeded in alienating women, who reject feminism out of fear that men will find them unappealing, the fantastic (jelly) belly dancers have no choice but to turn their focus on those who should embody all they stand against: straight men.

We have already experienced the wonders of feminist activism to persuade men to adore fat women. Next stands the cancer's insistence on "teaching" men to be good pink knights for the cause. Initially, this can be seen in the "4 Ways Men Are Taught to Objectify Women From Birth," article by Robin Tran, who once was a man, or may have a nuanced view of sexual identity. In a break from my usual behavior, I will use this person's preferred pronouns, despite transgenderism being a bizarre form of mental illness in its own right. Miss Tran's interesting perspective does shed further light on the ridiculous premises of the article however, as we shall quickly see. The third paragraph provides an immediate trove of feminist gold: "When we're taught that an entire gender exists purely to satisfy others' needs, it dehumanizes millions of people, and it's very difficult to have empathy for someone that you don't view as a real person."[28]

It might be entirely appropriate to label such prose as the work of a moron, but let us not stoop so low. First of all, women make up 76 percent of public school teachers, according to the National Center for Education Statistics,[29] so over two-thirds of the United States' students in public schools are taught by women. Of the entire school-going population, only 10 percent attend private schools according to the Council for American Private Education[30], meaning most children will grow up being taught by women. As an

[28] Tran, R. (2016, June 19). 4 Ways Men Are Taught to Objectify Women From Birth [Web log post]. Retrieved from http://everydayfeminism.com/2016/06/men-taught-to-objectify-women/

[29] Fast Facts. (n.d.). Retrieved from https://nces.ed.gov/fastfacts/display.asp?id=28

added tidbit, of the 12 million single parent households reported in the country in 2015, 80 percent were headed by single mothers,[31] further reinforcing the likelihood that the majority of children grow up with women as central, if not primary, role models.

It is necessary to begin the following section with such data because feminists tend to propagandize by relying on belief in some monstrous, all-powerful, and white-bearded Patriarchy scheming to dispossess them of life, lubricant, and the pursuit of sex toys. Side note: should this body actually exist, I pray it lets up on market censorship so feminists are liberated from the normal and desirable realm of dating. If these facts are true, they suggest the boys being so sadistically indoctrinated to objectify and rape women are being force-fed their behavior by WOMEN THEMSELVES, not the cackling and palm-rubbing Pats.

Tran's lofty lament about one gender existing to satisfy another's needs is especially endearing for another reason. Feminists endlessly rail against traditional gender roles, the oppression of pregnancy (because it ruins their pro-sex bodies) and the need for sexual liberation, all elements setting up a peculiar dynamic. A woman, after all, has limited uses for a man if she is not in some real sense "The Opposite Sex." Pregnancy for instance was one of the classic reasons why women held a special status; we all know delivering a child is difficult, and men have respected this fact for thousands of years. But when women are taught pregnancy oppresses them and are encouraged to abort, they are symbolically rejecting their prime directive as humans, and by extension, the respect of men. What

---

[30] Council for American Private Education. (n.d.). Retrieved from http://www.capenet.org/facts.html

[31] Freeman, A. (2015, August 18). Single Moms and Welfare Woes: A Higher-Education Dilemma. *The Atlantic*. Retrieved from https://www.theatlantic.com/education/archive/2015/08/why-single-moms-struggle-with-college/401582/

reason should men have to take a seat at the table of equality when women have completely subverted themselves and turned against nature itself?

Even more problematic is the insistence of feminists that women can only be liberated by throwing off the proverbial shackles of virginity and becoming sexually adventurous. Articles like "I'm A Slut—And 100% Proud of It (So Stop Shaming Me Already)" help illustrate this very real issue. Or we have what Emily Ratajkowski, a model, was quoted as saying: "I had a male friend who said I don't get blowjobs because I think it's offensive. That view is disgusting; [oral sex is] empowering! Being in love and acting sexually on it in a million different ways is empowering. I love men's butts. I shouldn't have to feel embarrassed by that."[32]

For the sake of feminism, let us suspend our own inclinations and assume this initial proposal is reasonable. Women should be allowed to become sexually liberated and act like men do when it comes to pursuing intercourse. To further this point it is worth stating that men broadly speaking are less interested in long-term relationships than women, and the male psychology tends to view sexual conquests as a good thing to be lauded by his friends and associates. Men are also less emotionally involved in sex than women, hence their ability to move on from one partner to the next with relative ease.

By telling women to become sexually liberated and embrace the burning stream that is slutdom feminists are teaching them to act like men do, and approach sex the same way. So both men and women are now more open to sex for the sake of sex, without any regard to emotions, romance, or procreation. Put simply, feminists are whining about men objectifying women whilst instructing their followers to pursue a lifestyle that will

---

[32] Burton, C. (2015, September 25). COVER STORY: NEW LINES. *GQ UK*. Retrieved from http://www.gq-magazine.co.uk/article/emily-ratajkowski-we-are-your-friends-blurred-lines

inevitably lead to their objectification. There is no middle ground on this issue. When sexual intercourse becomes nothing else but a devoid exchange over drinks and drunkenness, the result will be a decline in the value placed on a woman. Period, but only the grammatical kind.

In order to narrow the scope, consider how men perceive the other sex. Contrary to what feminists believe, men do not care for "meaningful conversation" with women. This poorly-chosen title ingrained on the dating profiles of countless women in the modern age is a futile attempt at appearing "deep." When men seek profound or fulfilling discussion, they go to other men. The problem with the female sex is its penchant for snarky gossip, constant talking for the sake of complaining, and empty discussion. Women have an idea of good conversation which is fundamentally obsessed with their own stale conception of things, like what useless major they selected or the non-profit they receive paychecks from for browsing Facebook to find a new dick from 9-5. All such topics are hollow and uninteresting to the discerning male.

As women have forced themselves further into the realms classically reserved for men, there are increasing signs of resentment on the part of males who do not enjoy such foreign company. Good illustrations include the development of the "Man Cave," "Boys Weekend," and the gamer culture, which is hostile to females. A massive sigh of dismay will typically overtake a group of men when one member chooses to bring his wife or girlfriend to a male-oriented event. It is a simple fact of life that men do not enjoy the company of women in the ways feminists fantasize, no matter how vulgar or rough the modern specimens may be. Men require at a basic level the understanding that they are different from women; the only exceptions are popularly known as homosexuals, transwomen, and the mentally ill.

8. **Virgin Hostile**

Returning to the topic at hand, feminists have actually helped the objectification of women with their rancid antics, especially as evidenced in the assault on virginity. Some time ago the feminist organs of influence began preaching about how virginity is supposedly a tool used to control and commodify women. They argued it puts an unfair burden on women, while also ignoring hundreds of years of social evolution around the concept, and the role women played in its propagation. Virginity was introduced in part to control the naïve antics of young women, who would have destroyed civilizations with their promiscuous ways, and to grant them special status in society. Like it or not, virginity places value on women in the eyes of men that would otherwise not exist. Males can hunt, cook, and build on their own. The only relevance of women comes in the realm of reproduction, which must be controlled to avoid the thundering cesspool of single motherhood currently defacing Western Civilization. Virginity as an idea is what makes men take a step back from pursuing certain girls to marry their wife. Instead of objectifying a woman as a warm portal for twelve hours of fun each night, it exalts her as someone for life and a mother to his children. As long as the issue remains strong, women hold out to find a better man, rather than the bile and entrails inhabiting fraternity houses and local bars. Female purity will remain an unavoidable consequence of the imposition of virginity as a social standard because women know they are of lesser value once they visit whore central.

This is a fact: women are biologically designated to give birth to children, and conservative opinions have historically associated sexual intercourse with procreation. Should feminists succeed in wiping the slate clean so that men and women are but pigs in constant heat, they will simultaneously achieve their goal while destroying everything else due to short-sightedness. Woman are after all largely dependent on men financially for the duration of their pregnancies, and in the time period after birth. Now, self-worshiping feminists will slyly cut in at this point by arguing the government should pay for extended maternity leave so women are no longer reliant on men in this category. Of course such a solution only works if men are willing to go along with it, as there will never be enough females to fuel such a program through tax dollars. A further problem is the implications for female advancement; if men must work to fund maternity leave programs paid by the government—or at bare minimum pick up the slack from the absence of female co-workers—it is reasonable to assume they will be promoted or given wage increases, resulting in the widening of the so-called "Wage Gap." One could address the problem by requiring both the mother and father to take time off, but it still leaves single folks out to dry. More on this later in the book.

We should also consider the fact that men in general do not like to marry or commit to sexually promiscuous girls. Their predilection goes beyond socially-constructed norms to a basic evolutionary principle: if the female mate has or continues to engage with multiple males it increases the chance she may become pregnant from the seed of someone else. The male is threatened by this possibility, hence the protective and jealous traits modern women describe as being "too possessive" or "controlling." Even today, after decades of feminist indoctrination, men still become fiercely jealous and even violent when another male encroaches on their territory or flirts with their woman. The sluttier a female is, the less likely she is to receive such treatment from a man.

The other gorilla in the room (by this I don't mean feminists themselves, although it is a great metaphor) is the absorption of DNA from sexual partners by women who engage in unrestrained sex with multiple people. Recent reports have suggested that the spermatozoa inside male ejaculate is absorbed by a woman who engages in unprotected sex,[33] even if she is on the pill. The walls of the uterus are designed to assist in delivery of the

---

[33] Knapton, S. (2014, October 01). Could previous lovers influence appearance of future children? The Telegraph. Retrieved from http://www.telegraph.co.uk/news/science/science-news/11133203/Could-previous-lovers-influence-appearance-of-future-children.html

sperm to the eggs, but apparently the mere presence inside leaves a lasting mark. Basically, sluts and shores will carry the traits of their prior sexual partners and may even pass them on to their later children.

Were all these young fellows STEM PhD's it might be not such a bad thing, but as we well know the choice of women is far less selective. Simply for the thrill of rough sex and some domestic violence on the side, women will date criminals like Charles Manson, OJ Simpson, and El Chapo. To see an attractive girl hanging with Crips or MS13 gangbangers is normal in modern America, largely because such parasites represent the muttering excitement which the real world seems to lack for feminists. All those prim Johnny boys whose mothers taught them that women want gentlemen are thus left swimming in miserable chaos as they search for a way to ring up some overweight harlot in her mid-thirties desperate for financial romance to support her three mixed race kids after a lifetime of dick diversity.

One can hardly respect, with all these scientific realities to keep in mind, that any man would willingly desire to run into the arms of an empowered feminist woman. It is especially clear when dealing the machinations of the middle-aged women discussed in the previous paragraph. Evolutionary theory tells us that females are driven by instinct to select the strongest and most likely to survive and produce children. Mating with the runty deer does not help the doe, as her offspring are less likely to endure versus yearlings from the Great Stag. When applied to humans the context works, but only if women have a rational brain, which most lack. The highest quality male is the one she should mate with, but instead feminist-inspired philosophy makes her run around fellating and riding numerous poles in hopes one belongs to Prince Charming down the road, once work is harder to stomach and parties feel less appealing.

The issue is, at this point the decent men who would raise healthy children are disgusted by the antics of women and choose to abandon them for bachelorhood or the sweeter and more feminine varieties of the Third World. Panic mode initiates in the now certifiable Fat-Fems, and they begin going after the weakest, most pathetic men to swindle into marriage and child-rearing, while others cry themselves to sleep in the loving embrace of a lesbian vibrator. It helps explain why so many misfortunate Indian, Asian, and Hispanic men are marrying the desperate and empowered white or black land whales of our time: they have no other options.

9. Playing With Reality

Cancer as a disease is probably the most horrible because it tends to defy reality and common sense. While some behaviors and lifestyle traits are good breeding grounds for the sickness (i.e. obesity), there are also instances where the completely improbable become victims. Babies born in healthy environments develop tumors, organic food consumers are suddenly canceled out, and those with no family history of the disease are diagnosed out of the blue. It is a nasty truth, and one which makes society desperate for some form of cure. Compounding the issue of course is cancer's resilience to many modern treatments. Feminism is likewise resistant, but more towards reality and facts than anything else. Just as closely-affiliated liberals will spend hours screaming epithets and emotional barbs in the face of undeniable truths, feminists have an intolerance for the way things are that could move mountains if it were not always stumbling over the pink oodles of its own contradictions. Precisely this category helps explain the endurance of the movement against time, space, and logic.

A grand place to start is feminism's convoluted focus on the invented conspiracy that fashion companies somehow act deliberately to abuse young women through their pricing and sizing. A solid example lies in the ATTN video "Women shouldn't have to spend a fortune on bras."[34] The seamlessly-edited piece attempts to create conflict out of the fact that women's' underwear can be expensive, and some females experience difficulties fitting into the mass-manufactured bras you find in popular big box stores. Its overall impetus, and that of many responses by women, suggests there should be some dramatic action to change this terrible state of affairs. Such action, at least from the feminist point of view, translates as government-backed decisions, or laws to establish "underwear equality." Yes, feminists do subsist in this regrettable reality: it's too hard, so the government should do it for me. What they do not grasp is that the underwear industry—particularly for women—is an expensive and peculiar one. Bras are after all meant to give comfort and support to women for long hours at a time, so it follows that they are not simply thrown together by a factory full of greedy old capitalists.

In order to quell the likely maelstrom of outraged feminists unwilling to let a man comment on the pads covering their (somewhat hairy) udders, I will defer to the work produced by Cara Harrington in her "There's a Reason It's Hard to Find Cheap Bras" article. Harrington does a wonderful job presenting the facts which rather irritate the feminist proposal. A central point she anchors with is that all lingerie is handmade due to the craftsmanship needs. Such a fact hurls several large wrenches in the minds of those who believe simple fixes exist, as it is difficult to cheaply replace a function which requires so much skill. We are not talking about McDonalds cashiers here. The average lingerie designer must undertake four years of school, another point the passing pink gargoyles are probably unaware of. Materials are also quite costly due to the nature of specific fabrics that

---

[34] ATTN: Women shouldn't have to spend a fortune on bras. [Video file]. (2016, July 01). Retrieved from https://www.facebook.com/attn/videos/1082052741830184/

work to ideally absorb sweat and provide flexibility, with some running as much as $300.00 per yard, according to Harrington's research. She finishes the article by pointing out something direct and profound: "It takes multiple people working together to transform a few bits of lace, and couple pieces of wire, and some straps into a fully-realized undergarment that can hold, shape and support the body—not just once, but potentially dozens of times."[35]

Now that we have established the very real cost of the lingerie business, we might glance over feminism's romance with the State. When normal people have an everyday problem with something like expensive underwear, they typically will look for a solution, or create one themselves. In the case of bras, a clever woman might assemble her friends, pray five times in the direction of Gloria Allred's mansion, and crowdfund a startup dedicated to producing cheaper offerings for women. Still slicker girls might bust into the sexist engineering schools as majors and develop new machines to prevent the lingering bratastrophe. Solid examples of folks who pursued valuable change include Chuck Hull, the inventor of 3D printing technology, and Jake Zien, who created Pivot Power, a flexible power strip. Both fellows saw an inefficiency and tried to correct it through their own ingenuity, all with the desire to address an issue which no doubt many others struggle with regularly.

Feminists on the other hand have repeatedly demonstrated their inability to appreciate this dynamic. They invest years of time leading "awareness campaigns" or trying to throttle other people's rights to express themselves whilst bringing nothing else to the potluck. When they do offer solutions, it is reliably for problems that do not exist, apart from the webbed dungeons of their own heads.

---

[35] Harrington, C. (2016, March 29). There's a Reason It's Hard to Find Cheap Bras. *Teen Vogue*. Retrieved from http://www.teenvogue.com/story/cost-of-lingerie-explainer

10. The Vagina Tax

In point, let us examine the antics of pharmacy owner Jolie Alony in New York. As part of a response to a perceived higher cost for women when it comes to female-specific products, Alony established a 7 percent "tax" on male customers, calculated by granting all women a tax break. She cited the election of 2016 as reason to pursue such a policy, while also turning her pez dispenser mouth on the usual target: the wonderful "Wage Gap." We shall proceed to discuss this later on, but first it is worth examining the cognitive dissonance required to adopt such a position. In her interview Alony said: "We wanted to share that women deserve to get a break, and men deserve to be charged 7 percent more. Women are spending more in general, and we make less, so we deserve to have a break."[36]

Holy pepperoni. Before anything else can be released, the supposed "gender tax" which Alony's crowd likes to shrivel up over is an absolute load of bullocks. I previously discussed why women's' underwear is expensive; in the broader setting of the market, the higher prices are based on specific ingredients in the "girlie" products, and their demand, as *Reason.com* explains.[37] Furthermore, it is not hard to see why women's razors, for example, might be more expensive than those for men. For starters, women make up about 53 percent of the population in New York City and 52 percent in New York State. The overall margin between the two genders exceeds 700,000 statewide, suggesting there would logically be a higher demand for women's products than men's equivalents. Smart companies facing higher demand increase prices to make more money and cover the costs required to manufacture or purchase a specific product. Lest we forget another unfair social burden that

---

[36] Bruner, R. (2016, October 12). This Pharmacy Instituted a Controversial 7% 'Man Tax' to Call Out Price Discrimination [Web log post]. Retrieved from http://time.com/4528451/pharmacy-man-tax/

[37] Brown, Elizabeth. "The 'Pink Tax' Is a Myth." *Reason.com*. N.p., 05 Jan. 2016. Web.

oppresses women by making them appear more attractive, remember the overall level of shaving. Most men use razors to trim their facial hair alone, except for the homosexuals and their cosmopolitan associates. Women on the other hand use the fancy pink blades on their legs, arms, faces, behinds, armpits, and cradles of life (or herpes). Significant use of a razor tends to dull the edge, especially when performed on a regular basis, and thus burns through the supply faster. Consequently, women go out and buy more frequently, driving up the cost. If feminists committed themselves to the "Chewbacca swag" lifestyle, they might see the costs of razors and hair removal creams fall, while the prices of vibrators and asexual country clubs memberships would undoubtedly rise.

Jolie Alony is important here because her entire effort is a fundamental misunderstanding of economics, and therefore doomed to failure. Supposing a business owner desired to help end racial segregation in the Antebellum South; would they logically bar all whites from their convenience store, and risk alienating large swaths of the population simply to get that point across? Highly unlikely. A clever person would welcome all different kinds in an effort to boost the store's revenue and force competitors to play along or lose money. This is the free market at work: compete or fall behind. Alony might have achieved this by making her store sales tax free for everyone, in effect pushing other pharmacies to do the same and perhaps impacting the laws on the books as well. Instead she chose to alienate half of the state's population, running the risk of turning them strongly against her business, and causing it to fail. Assuming she employs women, bankruptcy and closure would be a lot worse for her employees than paying slight premiums on the products they willingly choose to buy. As with the lingerie fiasco, feminists do not want to find independent, private sector solutions to their problems; they think the state should get involved.

11. Taking and Taxing

As long as the dull machinations of the government are in our ears we can fact-check the claim made by feminists about women paying more. Anyone in the possession of a rational mind can see how ridiculous this is. Each time a conservative politician forms his cabinet they will complain about lack of women chosen, and make similar bones about corporate CEOs or legislature membership in general. Keep in mind that men have been serving in combat roles in the United States for over 200 years, and lost millions of their gender in both world wars. The deaths of women were comparatively minor in the same conflicts. Men also have to register for Selective Service, a requirement you will rarely hear feminists squawking about, save when it concerns standards for women in the military. As we well know, when women are held to male standards they invariably fall flat on their A-cups or washout completely. An entire generation may have been weaned on Ridley Scott's *GI Jane*, but that movie was entirely fictional and not a reflection of reality.

To the central point, a study from New Zealand found that men paid in far more than women to the tax system while receiving fewer benefits.[38] The average woman is a net

---

[38] Bloomfield, J. (2016, August 16). Reblog: Research find that as a group, only men pay tax [Web log post]. Retrieved from http://judgybitch.com/2016/08/16/reblog-research-find-

taker, and will rack up a lifetime fiscal negative of $150,000 during her walk on earth. Men as a group will pay more taxes than their female counterparts because they work longer hours on average and do not enjoy eligibility for the same benefits women partake in. Males are also heavily represented in dangerous lines of work, such as coal mining and the lumber industry, while women are unlikely to pursue such professions. In other words, men put more into the economy while withdrawing comparatively little, even if they are on average in greater danger as a whole. Women are net takers, undermining the feminist suggestion that they occupy a disadvantaged place in society.

This data also helps explain why the same empowered divas who constantly harp on about the need to combat "The Patriarchy" and "Male Privilege" are the first in line to vote for politicians who expand state powers and feed the ever-growing welfare programs. Individuals who lack any significant stake in the system are bound to vote for increased expenditures because they will not suffer the consequences. In every recent election across multiple Western countries, unmarried women, the demographic most prized by feminist schemers in their propaganda campaign, have voted in huge majorities for leftist parties that support welfare and theft through taxation. Understanding this pattern in undeniably key to capturing the contours of the feminist agenda; they do not seek any real fix to the problems facing their countries, only easy enrichment for themselves.

The inability of feminists to grasp the reality behind actual statistics is nearly as problematic as their insufferable tendency to blame every failure by women on some abstract, but male-created force. If we take, for instance, the battle of over corporate gigs and female leadership the field becomes crystal clear. Since the glass ceiling was fractured by giants like Meg Whitman and Carly Fiorina with varying results, feminists have taken it upon themselves to warn helpless ladies about the supposed conspiracies afoot in big

that-as-a-group-only-men-pay-tax/

business. Whitman as an example is held in high regard for her service as CEO of ebay, as well as a more recent stint heading Hewlett-Packard. She made an impressive career for herself and later sought the governorship of California as a Republican, self-funding to the tune of $140 million. I certainly see that as poor investing sense, but as a multi-billionaire Whitman probably saw it as just another waltz with human experience, even after losing by nearly 14 points. While no doubt imperfect, she remains admirable for her achievements, which outpace most women who duck around under the feminist label.

Enter Carly Fiorina. Besides sharing status as a failed political candidate in California—as well as nationwide—Fiorina also took the role as CEO of Hewlett-Packard, only years before Whitman. During her tenure HP experienced a prolonged downturn, lost substantial market value, and ultimately had to send the California fighter a pink slip. In case anyone fears some sexist firing process, Fiorina walked away with a $20 million golden parachute, a nice consolation prize for her damage-doing in the capitalist world. Whitman received praise from some feminists, her politics aside. Fiorina on the other hand was one of the first to be christened with the "Glass Cliff" designation, a category of women supposedly setup to fail after men have run a company into the soil. Yet another example of strong, empowered women falling prey to the powers beyond their control. As they might say, she was spanked.

Yeah, right. Forget that HP was doing well when Fiorina took over, but saw its stock fall 50 percent during her tenure while experiencing incredible numbers of layoffs, and not in a terrible economy. Ignore the fact that shares rallied on her way out, and every move she attempted crumbled miserably. Whitman succeeded because she was a strong, independent woman. Fiorina failed because everyone hates women. That is the ludicrous proposal of feminists and their cancerous ilk.

Just to seem adequate, think back to the controversy surrounding the quick demise of Ellen Pao as CEO of Reddit. Pao experienced an especially stormy tenure as leader of the social media company due to policy changes she helped promulgate, including tighter controls on speech and discussions, as well as increased moderator powers. The smiling, retro-glasses wearing chick cut her time short by resigning, only a few years after filing a sexual harassment lawsuit against her previous employer. Most rational people called Pao out for her abject failure, but feminists refused to run or cheer the mainstream derby. They brought out the fullest rage of blog posts and internet videos to defend Pao, attempting to distract from her leadership by considering it the victim of misogyny and online bullying from 4chan and the "manosphere."

In reality, which we already know feminists refuse to accept, Pao was an atrocious example of female leadership. She angered and alienated her customer base by taking needless political positions and trying to turn Reddit into something it was not. The traditional user community was hostile to such shifts in managerial practice, creating the backlash which forced her out. That is simply the destiny of the business world. You win or you lose. Some people triumph, and others eat eggshells from the market gutter. Nothing is meant to be fair or progressive unless it specifically serves the business model.

Alas, the feminist refrain does not get any quieter. Writing in the illustrious *Guardian* newspaper, Jessica Valenti laid the blame for Pao's untimely fall on the Silicon Valley warrior's feminism. She wrote: "It's clear though, that what made Pao a target wasn't solely her gender; She wasn't just being attacked for being female, but for being a feminist."[39] As Nicholas Cage might say, "You don't say?" It's pretty obvious Pao was attacked for that main reason, at least insofar as her management record is concerned. The

---

[39] Valenti, J. (2015, July 17). Ellen Pao isn't harassed because she's female. It's because she's a feminist. The Guardian. Retrieved from https://www.theguardian.com/commentisfree/2015/jul/17/ellen-pao-harassment-feminist

problem with the Ellen Paos of the world is that they run about assuming those high fangled ideas which they hatch in the corridors of Ivy League echo chambers are somehow good prescriptions for society at-large. As it turns out, reality does not ping back the same ideas without criticism like elitists would prefer. Of course we know the response exhibited by the users, and it should surprise no one. Valenti includes information in her article by alluding to the population of teenage males in online comment sections, which are themselves breeding grounds for less-than-civil attacks and internet trolling. Instead of simply taking this as a dynamic that has colored social media since its inception, the Paoists see it as their mission to rise up and advocate against the issue. But as grand as everything may look from the lofty social justice perspective, you cannot run a successful business by excluding core customers in favor perspiring communists and feminist goblins.

Before going forth to the ultimate bonanza I want to cover two more instances of feminist pantomime convulsions over the disappointing performances by female leaders in the business sector. I will not suggest those ladies failed because they were women, but rather show how feminists refuse to accept that perhaps their hopes are not what fantasy makes them out to be. First off, we come to the marvelous tale of Marissa Mayer, current CEO of Yahoo. When Mayer took the reins as company leader in July 2012 she was lauded as an accomplished and attractive sign of Silicon Valley's crumbling wall of male supremacy. The young and photogenic Mayer secured a tremendous salary for her service, quelling any suggestions she was bought off cheaply due to the appearance of her sexual organs. If and when Mayer leaves her post early she will be entitled to $55 million in compensation, not too shabby in the shadowy world of men.

Now let us examine her record. In 2014, two years after she took command, Yahoo was pulling in $7.5 billion, not incredible but a far cry from abject destitution. Fast forward one year. Yahoo lost $4.4 billion, and continues to struggle as it looks for potential buyout offers.[40] Will feminists take ownership? Absolutely not. In the *Washington Post*, Jena McGregor went for the jugular, ascribing Mayer's experience to the aforementioned "Glass Cliff," the popular excuse for incompetent female CEOs. Bear in mind that Mayer led the company in a $1.1 billion acquisition of Tumblr, a fad social network site dominated by left-leaning whackjobs and immature adults. Tumblr in general has been eons ahead of the progressive spectrum, promoting such perversions as the Furry Fandom and the mental illness of multiple genders. The website failed to deliver additional revenue, yet that did not stop McGregor from starting up the printing presses of denial: "But others will say that Mayer, like other women before her in technology, was dealt a tough hand in the first place, accepting a particularly precarious role known as the 'glass cliff'."[41]

How convenient. Remember Steve Jobs being kicked out of Apple, only to return and do what his detractors never dreamed of? How about Donald Trump's comeback following an economic downturn in the 1990s? Over history countless men have been dealt "tough hands." Some succeeded, and others failed, but nowhere did you find countless articles shifting the blame to some hidden conspiracy to set-up males for downfall. And even if such a scheme existed, what does it say about the women falling prey to the various elements involved? If the mere offer of easy cash entices educated women to fall on their own swords then how much better are they versus the old guard of corrupt patriarchs who supposedly fixed the system?

---

[40] Greenfield, D. (2016, May 03). WHY WON'T ANYONE TALK ABOUT WHAT A TERRIBLE CEO MARISSA MAYER IS? *Front Page Mag.* Retrieved from http://www.frontpagemag.com/point/262704/why-wont-anyone-talk-about-what-terrible-ceo-daniel-greenfield
[41] McGregor, J. (2016, July 18). As Yahoo sale nears, do women in tech get pushed more onto the 'glass cliff'? *The Washington Post.* Retrieved from https://www.washingtonpost.com/news/on-leadership/wp/2016/07/18/as-yahoo-sale-nears-do-women-in-tech-get-pushed-more-onto-the-glass-cliff/?utm_term=.42d600ae9b3e

In addition, feminists seem to think women should be given good companies to run so they do not face challenges which might eclipse their shine. This is an immense contradiction. Women who are capable and equal to men do not need special conditions preassembled by men in order to find success. They will simply endure and find a way through the muck to emerge triumphant. Anyone who demands their job be secured in advance so success is guaranteed is lazy and pathetically inept. When one pauses to think however, those are both characteristics of feminists.

Perhaps the most stunning example of hypocrisy in the glass cliff category is visible in the saga of Elizabeth Holmes and Theranos. Back in 2014 Holmes emerged as the subject of countless article and television segments due to her apparent self-made status. Biographies glowed about her victory against early odds, a teenage prodigy who managed to develop advanced computer programs before launching her brainchild, the company Theranos. Considered groundbreaking, Theranos pioneered a cheap and quick alternative to mainstream blood testing at pharmacies, and Holmes soon garnered partnerships with major chain companies like Walgreens, as well as billions in venture capital funding. Big names quickly signed on, including retired Marine Corps general James Mattis and other prominent public figures. Part of Theranos' success was no doubt due to Holmes herself, whose blonde-haired, blue eyed appearance tucked inside a black turtleneck ala Steve Jobs endeared her to many hopeful people. She stood out among most entrepreneurs and businesspeople, quickly soaring to billionaire status in *Forbes* magazine and becoming one of the first women to attain such wealth from self-made means. The die was tossed.

Predictably, the feminists rang their bells of success. Holmes was swiftly elevated as a model for young girls and a cleaver to the classic mold of corporate America. Articles poured out in service of this objective, painting the blonde baroness as the herald for a new era of estrogen-fueled leadership to replace the dry, male-centric morass of business executives.

Like all things that are too good to be true, Holmes' story nosedived against reality. Investigations were initiated into the viability of the blood testing technology, questions were raised about Theranos' practices, and ultimately the CEO herself was barred from operating a laboratory for three years. On top of all this, declining fortunes for the company resulted in Holmes' net worth being listed as negative after Theranos' valuation sunk from $4.8 billion to less than $800 million. Sometime later, she would be charged with fraud by the Securities and Exchange Commission. By any fair estimation, Holmes was an absolute disaster as leader over the degenerating organization that is Theranos.

Not to worry though, for feminism has a brilliant solution to these particular problems. Holmes herself chose to imply to *Fortune* magazine as the controversy over Theranos unfolded that media coverage of her verged on sexism: "Until what happened in the last four weeks, I didn't understand what it means to be a woman in this space. Every article starting with, 'A young woman.' Right? Someone came up to me the other day, and they were like, 'I have never read an article about Mark Zuckerberg that starts with 'A young man.'"[42]

Yes, that is an actual statement by a CEO as her company is in the midst of blistering legal and economic problems. Let us focus on the way the media covers your leadership, not the actual quality and outcomes related to it. The mystical and pervading force of Patriarchy continues to wreak havoc, but on feminist women only. Thus in the instances of scandals at Enron or WorldCom, both run by men, the standard does not apply,

---

[42] Bellstrom, K. (2015, December 10). Elizabeth Holmes Hints at Sexism in Media Coverage. *Fortune*. Retrieved from http://fortune.com/2015/12/10/elizabeth-holmes-sexism-theranos/

because the scams specifically target budding women leaders. Men are simply corrupt by default, women due to conspiracy.

12. Female Leadership and Reality

The greatest red herring when it comes to a debate on female leadership is the assumption that they are discriminated against simply because of their sex. We already can imagine the specific biological problems that could serve to stymie a woman's ability in the workplace. Women often take off time when tending to newborn children, and may have to dalliance with periodicals that jar their comfort and mental state. Anyone who has spent time around a woman while she is on her period will attest to this, and it is a fair reason to justify why there has been great resistance to allowing women in combat zones, where such struggles might not be conducive to morale and unity.

A much greater factor is the high level of mental illness rates among women. According to a study in the United States, Europe, and the United Kingdom Commonwealth, women are 40 percent more likely to develop a mental illness, a stunning finding after endless feminist shrieking about the abilities of the gentle sex. The same study concluded women are 75 percent more likely than men to report depression, and 60 percent more likely to experience an anxiety-based disorder.[43] All these elements present a far stronger explanation for the fecklessness of women atop major business institutions. The stress of running operations for a massive corporation is certainly fair foundation to support significant personal issues with approaching others and resolving workplace related issues. Someone wrapped up in the fuss of pregnancy is hardly going to be effective running a leviathan of endless responsibility on a daily basis, nor the same while watering the planet

---

[43] Ball, J. (2013, May 23). Women 40% more likely than men to develop mental illness, study finds. *The Guardian*. Retrieved from https://www.theguardian.com/society/2013/may/22/women-men-mental-illness-study

with allegedly harmless red water every month. And it goes without saying that someone's damaged or sick mental state will handicap their own ability to process the magnitude surrounding a senior leadership job. All good leaders are standards for what should be the normal performance of their workers. If they are brought down by the fact of mental disability or derangement, then someone else entirely should be considered for the role of CEO.

13. The Wages of Deception

It necessarily comes to pass in our journey to the center of the feminist flab that we must deal with the matter of the "Wage Gap" promoted by their movement. The Wage Gap has been an article for conflict for a long while, first developing its wings in the 1970s during the push to enact the Equal Rights Amendment, an atrocious legal creation which was thankfully defeated by the common sense of the American people, including millions and millions of women. Ever since the ERA'S defeat feminists have gone on the warpath against their insatiable enemy, but the fractured edges inside their ranks remained insurmountable until recently. With the advent of the Tumblr age and the rise of leaders like Barack Obama, the pink pigitas were suddenly imbued with the needed cover to promulgate their myths to the populace. I will pause here to point out an important aspect of feminism. Despite constantly screeching their heads off about the ill effects men have on society, they use weak and emasculated males to advance their agenda. Solid examples in recent history include Prime Minister Justin Trudeau of Canada, who famously answered a question about why he chose to have a gender equal cabinet by saying "Because it's 2015."[44]

---

[44] Durando, J. (2015, November 05). Canadian PM Justin Trudeau says cabinet is half women 'because it's 2015' *USA TODAY*. Retrieved from

Back to the issue at stake, feminists have managed to brainwash large swaths of the female population into the idea there is some massive crisis in the American economy resulting in their pay being on average lower than men. You'll typically hear them smattering the public's ears with complaints about "78 cents" on the dollar, or bring up statistics which seem to suggest women are at a disadvantage when it comes to wages and job choices. Feminist publications tend to blame this on several different problems, which we will examine and refute one at a time.

To start, activists pursuing the Wage Gap frame will reliably mention the social and cultural factors playing into female disadvantage when it comes to the workplace. They blame social attitudes and gender norms for the low level of enrollment by women in STEM programs, which supposedly contributes to girls feeling they cannot stack up in an environment dominated by men. Thus feminists have had to pleasure us with immature campaigns such as the #ILookLikeAnEngineer hashtag on Twitter, ostensibly meant to fight stereotypes that engineers are predominantly male. Interestingly, you will never see feminists protesting about the number of female registered nurses (92 percent of the total[45]) or public school teachers, who we already know are 76 percent non-male.

Regardless of these statistics, one must ask why feminists feel compelled to push so hard against reality. If men dominate an area, intelligent (i.e. non-feminist) women can try on their own volition to rise up and break the mold. Arguing for special awareness campaigns only hammers home the suggestion that they are seeking preferential treatment. Recall that men simply evolved into positions to help them solve particular problems, while women largely became mothers and housekeepers by their own choice, due to a simple

http://www.usatoday.com/story/news/nation-now/2015/11/05/prime-minister-canada-women-cabinet-justin-trudeau/75207820/

[45] United States, Department of Labor, Bureau of Labor Statistics. (2008). *Quick Facts on Registered Nurses (RNs)*. Retrieved from https://www.dol.gov/wb/factsheets/Qf-nursing-08.htm

biological calculus and drive. Men are less likely to be the primary keepers of children due to their inability to give birth and nurse. In the scope of nature, societies will inevitably divide along the lines of private and public utility, where only those who contribute a specific benefit towards the whole are likely to have time free for research and personal development. Women who remain pregnant or spend their life taking care of children are less likely to pursue an education because their priority is motherhood.

It is not a matter of women being wholeheartedly incapable of engaging with advanced math or science; they simply ought to be understood to have come from a different background and permitted to rise based on their own abilities, rather than political pressure. The alternative is something destined to dumb down the quality of education.[46] Just as Affirmative Action tends to send unqualified people to elite colleges and jobs, pressure groups focused on boosting the quota of women in particular fields will have the same effect. Say a given college wants to increase the representation of women in its engineering program. A proper approach would be to go hunting for recruits by seeking out the top performing ladies in high school science and mathematics. This ensures only individuals with decent talents apply, while also strengthening the college's popularity as a whole.

Not a chance. Instead the academic world is subjected to forced campaigns both at the macro and micro social levels intended to compel institutions to change their ways. Problem is, girls do not typically pursue STEM subjects to begin with, and often fail out from engineering courses because they are fundamentally unable to handle the demands of those classes. There is not conspiracy behind such a fact, and many men are no better at

[46] Groom, N. (2017, January 24). 'What a disaster': Top scientist says high school physics is being 'feminised' - with difficult equations taken out of exams to make the subject more appealing to girls. Daily Mail. Retrieved from http://www.dailymail.co.uk/news/article-4151966/Michelle-Simmons-says-HSC-curriculum-changes-horriying.html#ixzz4YEAD4nBF

grasping the concepts required to succeed in Electrical or Mechanical engineering. The pool of individuals majoring in the field is already small, precisely because it is not a cakewalk. When feminists unveil their new array of weaponry they invariably send the message that their intent is on dramatically reshaping the education system to fulfill a cancerous political ambition.

While we can probably get away with allowing less rigor in programs for the liberal arts, doing so to STEM programs means less qualified graduates operating inside industries where precision is critical. Electronics engineers for example have to employ immense degrees of patience in order to accurately solder parts to a circuit board and other pieces of hardware. Mistakes brought on by poor workmanship or instruction of students can result in massive structural problems with the finished products, which oftentimes support critical systems in healthcare and public safety. For this reason having a robust, uncompromising policy concerning educational standards is imperative.

As a solid indication of feminist haplessness on the issue, consider the following image[47] propagated throughout the internet to support female participation as STEM graduates. It depicts a happy young brunette holding a soldering iron and focusing her efforts upon a circuit board. Initially meant to draw women into the STEM field, it soon became the center of flagrant mockery for the obvious lack of understanding regarding basic safety, as the girl is holding the iron with her bare hands, guaranteeing serious burns from the heat if it was actually being used.

---

[47] Feminist own goal [Web log post]. (2016, March 17). Retrieved from http://didactsreach.blogspot.com/2016/03/feminist-own-goal.html

Once again, feminism is more concerned with the vague exterior, the opaque window hiding an empty home. The mere visibility of a certain percentage of creatures with female sex organs must necessarily trump common sense and the needs demanded by society for safety and security. What is particularly heinous about this mindset lies with the consequences native to women in those fields who pursue them in their own merits. If the STEM arena is flooded by underqualified women like feminists desire, the effect will be a lowering of standards that will disadvantage those ladies seeking to challenge themselves in real ways. The decline in rigor also stands to increase repair and revision costs as the airheads make grave errors in their craft and blame it all on "Patriarchy," and the "Glass circuit board."

Back to the Wage Gap, another line frequently cast out concerns women making less than men across broader market and industry averages. There are several reasons why this appears to be the case, but none have to do with a systemic attempt at swindling women out of their own money. For one, women make less than men because they make different life choices and approach problems from a varied perspective. A primary contributing factor to the disparity in compensation is poor negotiating skills on the part of women, who are by nature demure and submissive. Faced with low-balled salary offers, the average woman is incapable of utilizing requisite abilities to ensure she receives the maximum starting level of compensation. Women tend to dither and become intimidated at the prospects surrounding a salary negotiation,[48] resulting in them falling back and losing out. On the other hand, men stay cool under pressure and are more inclined to force an issue if it leads to higher starting pay.

A simple enough solution to the issue resides in the empowerment of women to become effective at negotiation, as well more assertive. Girls might take classes to hone their interpersonal talents, or assume leadership roles to help strengthen their resolve. As per usual, feminism insists on government action to rectify the problem rather than using the rules of private society as the grounds for a fix.

Next there is the issue underpinning pay discrepancies beyond all else: life choices. Take for instance the examples of two employees who started working at the same company at the time, at age 26, one male, one female. They are hired at the same rate because they have equal qualifications and due to the employer policy against any sort of wage negotiation for starting salaries. Our two heroes, Bobby and Mary, proceed to work two years while remaining in good standing with the company.

Everything good, right? Not exactly. You see, Mary leads an active romantic life for most of her twenties, attaining the liberation and emancipation she craves through orgasms. Bobby on the other hand is a helpless incel who works hard but has nothing besides a Waifu pillow and modified My Little Pony plush doll at home to make merriment

[48] Breslin, S. (2011, August 4). Why Men Are Better Negotiators Than Women. Forbes. Retrieved from http://www.forbes.com/sites/susannahbreslin/2011/08/04/why-men-are-better-negotiators-than-women/#3c1476fe3fcd

with. As Mary nears thirty she freaks out; she needs a man, and only Stanley, the nerdy and financially stable office accountant is available. Stan in floored by Mary's portly beauty, and while she is unimpressed by the level of shine off his mostly bare forehead, they soon get married. This occurs at age twenty-nine, and Mary's heavy consumption of *Keeping Up With The Kardashians* drives her to get off birth control. Nine months later she lets loose a loud broadside and pops out gender indeterminate Clarencia, and then proceeds to request maternity leave.

At this point things become complicated. Due to the time Mary is taking off, Bobby's projects lack the support they once knew because of Mary's presence. In this situation the company has two primary options: one, make existing employees work much harder to cover the gap, at this point to the detriment of Bobby, who has to put in more time at his salaried rate, or hire a temp. The latter option is not highly desirable, as hiring is costly and it can be difficult to find individuals who are interested in a purely temporary role.

It should be obvious that Bobby is not to blame for Mary's pregnancy; after all, he is an incel. Mary made a conscious decision to grow a baby inside her belly, and must live with the consequences of her decision. Bobby cannot have babies himself, so under the doctrine of equality it is ridiculous to subject him to additional labor without a tangible incentive. Some options could include overtime pay, a raise for extra effort, or perhaps a promotion. Any of these elements would necessarily result in Bobby's average pay rising above Mary's assuming she has not previously surpassed him. The point is, the Wage Gap will continue to prevail as long as women make the same decisions about childbirth as they have in the past.

Alternatively we might take the approach of the extreme equalitarians who demand both men and women be forced to take off time when their baby is born. Here the basic logic argues that both parts in the couple taking leave means they each suffer the detriment to their career, thus helping diminish the effects of inequality between the sexes. In this case, problems do not exactly go away. For every couple taking time off, how will the company or companies survive? We have already explained how temporary employees are expensive and difficult to attain, yet here the problem is only exacerbated as managers struggle to find coverage for their lost productivity. Once again Bobby and others like him will be working harder and longer, yet feminist dictums insist they be paid the same as the women who are taking time off for unequal work. Sexism and discrimination is ok, as long as the victim is an expendable male.

Succeeding this point we have the women who elect to leave work entirely for years at a time in order to care for and raise their children. When the mistresses of propaganda conjure up their Wage Gap statistics they reliably fail to control the effects of individual women and their choices on the economy at-large. If a woman takes the extended time off route after her delivery and leaves the industry for a year or more, when she returns her pay will naturally be lower than the gentleman who was hired by her side. Unfair? Hardly. Childbirth is a specific choice for all but rape victims, yet the feminist brain tumor views it as just one more bump on the road to Chief Executive Officer.

Once more we do not see the flamingoes crying out that men who leave the workforce to tend to their families or personal health issues are not paid the same as the ones who stayed if they return at a later date. Most if not all industries operate on the basis of experience level. A strong, liberated feminist will not, presumably, hire the roofing contractor with one year experience, unless he is a poor, oppressed Muslim immigrant from Somalia. She will rather turn to the armpit-unshaven, tough-as-stilettoes contractor woman with twenty-five years experience and an army of semi-documented Chicanas in tow. The main idea is of course that experience has a higher correlation with quality of craftsmanship and work, and thus can command a higher fee. For most folks, including many feminists, it is a perfectly reasonable thought process. They simply choose to ignore common sense when it comes to women, because intolerance and Patriarchy. As for men? Their fate can be left to the sharks, because some majestic marine power has been helping them the entire time.

When the data is compiled properly, women are not nearly as bad of as claimed. For instance, men work on average 15 percent longer than women do over their lifetime, and are more likely to select dangerous jobs in uncomfortable places.[49] They also pursue more challenging specializations and demands at work,[50] boosting their lifetime earnings versus those of females, all this while having less access to government programs like women enjoy.

Given how it has been shown that women are net takers in terms of government services, one might logically assume feminists would seek some form of drastic change to ensure their sisters become producers, and not only producers of sarcasm. To the point, feminists should get their cottage cheese legs off of the ergonomic chairs at the BuzzFeed office and actively start companies operating under the equal pay system. They can offer luxurious healthcare with low monthly premiums, and paid leave packages to ensure both halves or partners have the ability to provide and will not support Patriarchy. Wages could be fixed at a $15.00 minimum and women encouraged to apply for top positions even if they have less experience than male counterparts. Sexual harassment would likely go away entirely as an issue with women holding steady at the helm. It would all be marvelous, part business and part political activism.

---

[49] Tobak, S. (2011, March 08). The Gender Pay Gap is a Complete Myth. Retrieved from http://www.cbsnews.com/news/the-gender-pay-gap-is-a-complete-myth/
[50] Ibid.

Unfortunately, we cannot have nice things. Despite the endless enunciation over needs for change in society you can rest assured the feminist poltroons are focused on the state, and the state alone. This legislation or that, tax increases or resolutions, feminists will always argue it is up to the government to effect change on society, not people themselves. What most puzzles the brain in this case is the degree to which the fem phalanx has agreed to throw itself prostrate (or prostate?) before the most patriarchal institution in history. After all, it is the state which enforced anti-suffragette laws and levied the property rules to disenfranchise women. The state also restricted where and how long women were permitted to work, cutting a swath against anxious liberators.

14. The Greater Feminist Psychosis

Though it is difficult to pinpoint exactly, I will continue to advance the following theory in regards to the matter: no matter how they portray themselves in public or at work, many feminists secretly harbor a desire to be dominated, body and soul, by a man. Whether they appreciate the suggestion or not, the state is an embodiment of what they believe should not exist: absolute power, the capacity to be rough and violent, and a financial provider. These are all traits which strong, empowered women must reject outright by feminist principle, yet they lust after a colossus-like savior who can rush in, protect them, and restore order within the muttering existence they know. Feminists are naturally weak in constitution as well as personal bravery, hence their predilection for men who exhibit such qualities in natural, if not slightly hyped, ways.

We can see the extent to which feminist women fall into their own trap by considering the sexual habits they engage in. Anyone who has dated a feminist knows they are quick to surrender their pantaloons for the sweet justice that is sex. A couple drinks, or simply a guy with average charm, and they rush to insert a male appendage in one of their several orifices. It is actually quite comical. The same women who preach dignity for their gender and attack rape culture cannot wait five seconds before fellating a total stranger, or sticking his reproductive organ inside their rectum. Some writers dismiss such impulses as the joys of being a liberated woman, yet they fail to address the specific item at stake: female dignity. If these ladies are indeed so committed to self-respect then they would not go about in pursuit of activities that are at the very least hostile towards its maintenance. Placing a man's penis in their mouth is a distinctly symbolic act of subservience to him, and as one might imagine, it has become a testy subject in feminist circles. *Feministe* writer Jill Filipovic handles this in the awkward way expected with her "Feminist Politics of Blowjobs" article. In the piece Filipovic attempts to take a middle ground on the issue, while still conceding women have to be seen as feminists regardless of their sex practices. She notes: "I'm no fan of shaming women for their sexual choices. I think it's absolute bullshit to call one's feminism into question because she gives head, or because she enjoys BDSM, or because she engages in whatever other 'Patriarchy-approved' sex practice."[51]

But there is a problem. All of these activities fundamentally cut at the notion that women need to preserve their dignity under the feminist model. For instance, the doggy style sex position involves a man penetrating a woman from behind while slapping her buttocks and pulling her hair. The idea is to simulate the behavior of wild dogs while mating. By any rational standard, a feminist who engages in such behavior is severely undermining the goal of promoting respect for herself and other women.

It should still come as no surprise that feminists have resorted to pathetic normalization campaigns to avoid facing the contradictions of their politics and sexual proclivities. Romper's Lindsay Mack attempts such a reconciliation with her "7 Ways Doggy Style is Actually a Feminist Choice." Her arguments include that it gives women

---

[51] Filipovic, J. (2006, June 19). Feminist Politics of Blowjob [Web log post]. Retrieved from http://www.feministe.us/blog/archives/2006/06/19/feminist-politics-of-blowjobs/

control, added stimulation, and turns her on. All good things, but hardly the hallmarks of a successful liberation activist. Mack's most telling point is the fourth, concerning animalism. She says: "If you'd like to go at it like animals from time to time, that's totally fine."[52] In addition, she mentions the supposed hotness surrounding vulnerability.

Mack can be excused for her sexual desires, but her argument only files more holes in the bars of feminist logic. Why should women who regularly malign masculine men and the Patriarchy be granted a free pass to indulge in sexual practices that are at a minimum a compromise of feminist pride? Each time a feminist sucks a man's dick or is penetrated from behind she reinforces the same patriarchal concepts her other activities are meant to oppose. Dismissing it by using sexual expression as the key takes all responsibility away from hypocritical women who live double lives in the feminist column.

The worst manifestation of feminist cancer in the realm is the obsession with BDSM. While sex may have rough elements in general, BDSM employs an entire culture of people who worship at the altar of bondage and sexual humiliation. Individual participants will specifically seek out "dungeons" where they are restrained and forced to undergo intense physical and mental abuse. This can include being violently beaten while tied or cuffed, wrapped in a leather suit without ability to breathe, and choked by a partner. Much as it may seem justified under the guise of sexual empowerment, BDSM in general contributes to the same cultural norms which feminists claim to dislike, but are forced to explain away in the sexual realm.

Unsurprisingly, BDSM has also become a very touchy subject (pun intended) within the gardens of unshaven tarantulas. In an article on *The Frisky*, prolific writer on

---

[52] Mack, L. (2016, August 17). 7 Ways Doggy Style is Actually a Feminist Choice [Web log post]. Retrieved from https://www.romper.com/p/7-ways-doggy-style-is-actually-a-feminist-choice-16519

feminist issues Jessica Wakeman opens up about her experiences with such a form of relationship:

> "As part of our 'play,' I would ask him permission to do lots of things. I told him about all the kinds of bras and panties in my drawers and each morning he'd tell me which ones to wear, which I would send him in a photo. I would ask him how to dress each morning. I would ask him if I could watch a movie or if I had to work on writing a freelance article more. If I 'disobeyed' him during this sexy-talk 'play,' he would tell me over the phone or over IM how he would 'punish' me." [53]

One can sense while reading the paragraph both the relative moistness of the author and her surrender to abject hypocrisy. She goes on to discuss elsewhere[54] her love for dominant men, only stopping with the usual justification that it is a sexual fetish which does not reflect the way she lives life. All such spinning might work if Wakeman was restricting her interests to sexual activities, but clearly she is not. Any female who claims the mantle of feminism whilst engaging in a LIFESTYLE where every little question must be cleared with a dominant male who threatens corporal punishment in exchange for disobedience is clearly attempting to escape with perfect hypocrisy. Here we have more than simply the vestiges of carnal ambitions; a woman who makes a living lamenting the objectification of women by dominant men wants to be subjected to similar treatment. Bloody ridiculous.

Every step a person takes, from simple life choices to major career decisions, is driven fundamentally by the underpinning dynamic of representation. Just as women who

---

[53] Wakeman, J. (2010, March 02). Girl Talk: I Wanted To Be Dominated [Web log post]. Retrieved from http://www.thefrisky.com/2010-03-02/girl-talk-i-wanted-to-be-dominated/
[54] BDSM And Feminism: "Stop Telling Me What I'm Supposed To Like, D*mn It." [Web log interview]. (2010, October 17). Retrieved from http://jezebel.com/5666107/bdsm-and-feminism-stop-telling-me-what-im-supposed-to-like-dmn-it

preach feminist independence while living off the government are sheer hypocrites, the same Amazonians calling out the guards on sexist social practices while partaking in them should be the target of endless mockery. A feminist who desires to be ordered around, spanked, or otherwise violently restrained and taken is wallowing in streams of total treason to the movement.

I will remind at this point the role feminism plays, with all its cancerous glory, in repressing the natural inclinations carried by women. At the most fundamental level, females adore being objectified and dominated by masculine men. It harkens back to their evolutionary roots as wildings hunted down for mating by the strongest males. With the advent of feminism, small segments of the womanly coalition began to question their own normal desires as evil or wrong. These creatures revolted against what was widely practiced, in the process making themselves the most miserable and forsaken creatures in existence. Its malevolent nature helps explain why the fat, unclean, and poorly-groomed girls who take this viewpoint always look on with envy at their feminine colleagues, who undoubtedly will receive more attention from the opposite sex, and the accompanying satisfaction. The rejected women are thus left to scrabble hopelessly after their destiny, hoping that perhaps one day they will experience the happiness which only surrender to masculine domination can supply. Herein is the reason for feminist apologetics when it comes to BDSM: they are caught by their own biological directives and an invented idea of self-righteous political acceptability. They refuse to give up either one, but the incompatibility is slowly driving them mad, as we can see from the statistics on mental illness.

Before exiting this section there are two further matters to attend. First, the issue of *Fifty Shades of Grey*. Originally released in 2011, the travesty against good English prose aimed to get at female fantasies of absolute submission to a man who is rich, white, and virulently masculine. Normally any woman who engages in this manner of submissive relationship with these contexts would be viewed as a pathetic gold-digger, but this did not stop feminists from swallowing it like the other thick substances they frequently ingest on the road to defeating Patriarchy. With sexual domination however, comes a different message. The main female character, Anastasia Steele, is a cute but awkward English Literature major who accidentally ends up interviewing Christian Grey, a powerful and handsome billionaire who has nothing to do save make donations to charity and engage in violent sexual foreplay, with Steele as his current target.

Right here it is worth stopping to consider the facts while feminists get their fair trade typewriters reader. *Fifty Shades* has to be seen for what it is: a realization of the dreams held by many women, especially feminists. The characters are perfect vehicles to this end. Your typical feminist is a sad, uncertain nerd with low self-esteem who pursues an arts or humanities education. Her politics force her into a problematic struggle between what the Germaine Greers see as reasonable and their own soaking desires, which inevitably include being lost completely through orgasm to strong and impervious men. Anastasia is all of these things. She stumbles through her interactions with Grey, exchanging her cool exterior for hilarious internal put-downs of herself like "double crap!" while her moves fall stale on the high rise air. E.L. James' only real talent in her otherwise atrocious writing is to illustrate the hopelessness of Anastasia against Christian's lordly omnipotence. No matter what the girl does she ends up falling to Grey's spell. In the end her character submits utterly with a written contract and allows the billionaire Chad to slap her bottom all the way to China, Maoist red and all. Like it or not, Anastasia exemplifies feminists to a T. Wherever they are screaming to be uplifted and independent of men they can be found concurrently getting off to the thought of total domination, body and soul. They crave absolute surrender and servitude to the tender head on a massive phallus.

The final peg to the lumber of feminist hypocrisies rests with their troublesome salivation for the experience of rape. Recent years have brought forth the crimson tide of false rape accusations and crying appeals to end "Rape Culture," a vestige so void and meaningless it can be used in concert with other irrelevant ideas to batter any fool brash enough with his methods. Entire budgets have been dedicated to this supposed problem, and awareness campaigns spread hoping to teach boys not to rape, while allowing women the freedom of sexual exploration. Simply labeling a man as a rapist is enough to destroy his career, have him locked up, and render all defenses the handiwork of "victim blaming."

At a later point we will examine the hypocrisies embedded in the rape hysteria activists, but first there lies the matter of self-loathing and repressed feminists in this category. To start, the specific issue of rape fantasies must be focused upon. In her excellent "5 Reasons Women Love Rape Fantasies" article, Janet Bloomfield explains the various aspects feeding into the deranged female lust for rape: "Rape fantasies get to sidestep all these complicated 'how many dicks are too many dicks' questions by removing consent from the equation. No one in their right mind, surely, would count a rapist among a woman's numbers. She was taken. She cannot be held responsible. She's not a slut! She's a victim."[55]

Out-bloody-standing. The emphasis on desire for victimhood and powerlessness is a common theme we have observed from feminists thus far. Every issue labeled as "women's" is constantly described in terms which place women in oppressed positions despite their claimed superiority. Women are incapable of solving their own problems and must find a way to corrupt gullible men so they gain an otherwise elusive prayer. By removing responsibility from themselves these ladies effectively purge their movement of

---

[55] Bloomfield, J. (2015, February 18). 5 Reasons Women Love Rape Fantasies. Thought Catalog. Retrieved from http://thoughtcatalog.com/janet-bloomfield/2015/02/5-reasons-women-love-rape-fantasies/

any purpose save complaining and sniping individuals who are far more useful at accomplishing change.

Because women are in general inferior to men, the wiliest feminists amongst them have also turned rape fantasies into weapons of violence against males. Bloomfield reveals how the superior position of men on a social level relegates women to a weaker place. In order to strike above their weight, which feminists have copious supplies of, these ladies will invent reasons to mobilize effeminate men and the state against their hated targets. The response is a massive social army shrieking for death and rape towards any man even slightly associated with women and inequities.

15. Rape Battles

While we touch on the lilli pad of rape fantasies the feminist cancer has only grown larger, with its heart resting on a celebration of false rape accusations as a measure to achieve political aims. The issue came to prominence most notably in 2014, when *Rolling Stone* magazine published a tell-all story of one girl's experience being raped by frat house brothers at the University of Virginia. Thanks to the zealous female politics practiced by the author, Sabrina Erdely, claimant Jackie managed to launch nationwide controversy that led to the unjust persecution of fraternities as a whole, the erection of dangerous kangaroos courts in the media, and the slandering of UVA official Nicole Erano. Like the greedy parasites they are, the news media rushed for the juiciness afoot in the story without bothering to verify Jackie's claims. It was only due to the dedicated work invested by journalists like Chuck C. Johnson of *GotNews* that the falsehoods were uncovered, with the article found to be fabricated and Jackie exposed for her past false rape accusations.[56]

---

[56] Johnson, C. (2016, November 04). #RollingStoneTrial: GotNews & Chuck Johnson Bring Down Rolling Stone Over #JackieCoakley. Retrieved from http://gotnews.com/rollingstonetrial-gotnews-chuck-johnson-bring-rolling-stone-jackiecoakley/

It would be natural to assume a decent person might turn on this matter and reject the lies as destructive to the public, but feminists are a different group entirely. Instead of the logical move they chose the burning earth, launching articles justifying deception and thievery of the truth because it might ultimately serve to advance the fight against rape culture. If you are left puzzled by such a sniveling move, keep in mind the source from whence it springs. Women are, after all, vastly inferior to men in each category save child rearing. Feminists also rely heavily on the state to enforce rules that are completely unreasonable and surely sexist. Is it any wonder then that they see sexual assault as a weapon to bring down hated male targets? The proof, as they might say, is buried under eight kilos of feminist lard pudding. Since the law is the one vehicle on their side of the turf, the fembots utilize its tendrils to deal as much damage against men as possible, usually in cowardly manners.

Our next subject is Emma Sulkowicz, a person of questionable moral standing who attracted attention in 2013 after filing complaints with the Columbia University over her alleged rape at the hands of Paul Nungesser, an ex-boyfriend and fellow student. Sulkowicz contrived a substantial alibi together with her friends, who remained mostly anonymous, and soared to media fame. To better typify her dilemma, Sulkowicz launched an art project involving her lugging around the mattress she was allegedly raped on, including to her own graduation. The Ivy Leaguer's art project gained quick attention, leading to even more campaigns against gender violence and activism to prevent sexual assault. Sulkowicz was of course a hero in the minds of the satin sisters, and her prominence continued to rise with meetings alongside Kirsten Gillibrand, the senator from New York. Slowly but surely the Patriarchy appeared to be being washed away as courageous women came forth to support their poor and unfortunate sister. Some groups like the National Organization for Women even came out to award Sulkowicz for her activism and alleged bravery.

Alas, it was but lies. Within months of the story's birth, after violent prognostications by the media, facts began quietly emerging. For one, Sulkowicz's story started to fall apart. The alibis of her witnesses were brittle to begin with, and their anonymous nature resulted in more questions bubbling up from alternative news sites. Many wondered why the apparent victim refused to go to the police department right away instead of launching an obscure art project, particularly at so liberal a school as Columbia. Above all, Sulkowicz's own story lacked credibility after it was revealed she has been on the losing end of a relationship with Nungesser, and only went for the rape accusation once he made it clear he was moving on without her. Perhaps the most telling tidbit came in a message she sent him on Facebook reading: "Fuck me in the butt."[57] Besides a possible desire to reduce her own ability to sit down comfortably, Sulkowicz was communicating her full-throated desire to be Nungesser's sexual conquest, and continued believing in the possibility until things soured. In other words, her entire "rape" came as a result of her being dumped, a convenient new method for women to rid themselves of emotional hang-ups and regret which such raw relationships may bring. We will never know exactly what possessed her to make the decision, but the suggestions are fairly clear; either she felt guilty about her past life getting sodomized by Nungesser, or she was emotionally damaged by his abandonment. Whatever the case, she had to persuade herself it was morally right to ruin a man's life simply because he no longer wished for his penis to be inside her bottom. As though Sulkowicz's behavior was not already deranged enough, she chose to further her case for sectioning by acting in a softcore pornographic film with an overweight, possibly straight-for-pay actor to demonstrate how her rape could have moved from consensual to non-consensual sex in a short time period.

---

[57] Forney, M. (April 26). Student Accused Of Rape By Emma Sulkowicz To Sue Columbia University [Web log post]. Retrieved from http://www.returnofkings.com/62253/student-accused-of-rape-by-emma-sulkowicz-to-sue-columbia-university

No matter how many times it was shown that Sulkowicz was a liar, she steadily returned with the refrain of support from feminist organizations who defended her amidst the problem that is reality. Just in June 2016 Sulkowicz was awarded the Woman of Courage prize by the National Organization for Women. In predictably drooling terms, NOW's leadership bestowed on their designee a fantasy of a biography portraying her as everything her actions showed she is not, and thus helped to legitimize her own dishonesty. In the announcement organization president Terry O'Neil stated: "Sulkowicz did what many rape victims cannot do, she channeled her fear into a public demonstration and brought attention to her rapist's despicable act and highly inadequate punishment."[58] She goes on to say: "Emma is an inspiration to us all."[59]

If the feeling is one of absolute confusion, you may just be free the brain tumor which is modern feminism. There is absolutely no way for a person of sound mind to conclude Sulkowicz's actions are the things of inspiration, or an exhibition of courage. She deliberately embarked on a quest with the intent of ruining Paul Nungesser's life through the media as revenge for her relationship's spiral towards the earth. And how exactly is she in any sense a model for young women? A chick who sends Facebook posts begging to be "fucked in the butt" is hardly the sort you would want representing your family, or as the vessel to produce a fresh generation. To be fair, I accept most feminists have taken it upon themselves to reject traditional reproductive sex as tantamount to misogyny and rape, but perhaps once technology is advanced enough to allow gay men the ability to reproduce using their rectal cavity, feminists will jump on board to show solidarity with another

---

[58] Goldenberg, A. R. (2016, June 28). NOW Calls Girl Who Falsely Cried Rape an 'Inspiration' to Real Rape Victims [Web log post]. Retrieved from http://www.mrctv.org/blog/now-calls-girl-who-famously-cried-rape-inspiration-real-rape-victims
[59] Ibid.

persecuted class. Given the apparent fascination that feminists like Sulkowicz have with anal sex, it is not too terribly difficult to imagine.

16. Rape Hypocrisy

In our mission to understand the degree to which feminist cancer has overtaken hearts and minds we need consider the vaunted issue of contradictions when it comes to prevailing notions about Rape Culture. Anyone who has taken part in sexual assault awareness workshops or training will recall the popular 1 in 4 statistic concerning college-aged women who will be sexually assaulted. As sinister as it may sound, the study is largely based on a skewing of the definition regarding sexual assault. Only 11 percent of the women reporting said they had been sexually assaulted on the level equating criminal activity.[60] Unfortunately the premature triumphalists will rely heavily on such numbers in their quest to prove America's alleged succumbing to a world where rapists lurk around each corner. A pat on the behind by a drunk fraternity brother may be objectionable, yet it hardly matches the definition of rape. The does not stop the reporting class, and given that many are likely feminists themselves, we should expect the number of false reports to be astronomically high, particularly when women choose to call the last sex before a breakup "violent rape." That information is carefully excluded from every run-of-the-problem glasses article which bleeds forth from the bared fangs grafted to feminist loins.

Let us however be nice and accept the feminist proposition on rape campuses, and the broader rape epidemic. In one sense it makes us terribly flawed creatures deserving pure scorn, but at times one must look into the heart of the enemy, no matter how black and acidic their vitals may be. So rape is everywhere, and men love to rape. Boys must be

---

[60] Crocker, L. (2015, September 21). Why the New 'One in Four' Campus Rape Statistic Is Misleading. *The Daily Beast*. Retrieved from http://www.thedailybeast.com/articles/2015/09/21/how-misleading-is-the-new-one-in-four-campus-rape-statistic.html

taught to respect women and ignore their youthful drives in favor deep conversation that ends only as he carefully performs pleasure on her vagina using his mouth. Anything else bears the mark of Patriarchy, and thus cannot be permitted. Women should be treasured and uplifted in positions carrying immense power so the world can gradually move away from hateful intolerance towards the happily diverse, unending river of milk, honey, and lemon birth control, floating softly in the floes and waves of rich period blood. Then the world can have peace.

Were all these conditions met the world would still face an enduring problem, which feminists themselves seem entirely unwilling to solve. Their popular screech about men who question the intelligence of women who get wasted at college parties and make themselves vulnerable to sexual assault has been to cry "victim blaming," succeeded by ten Hail Glorias as they lament the corrupt state of Western culture. Some seminars will even require everyone, but especially men, to accept women going to any party, whether drunk or not, with the guarantee that they should feel safe. The underlying goal is to set the rules and prevent any logical thought process demanding more from girls than the slutted-up mentality of today. The real takeaway rests with fierce hostility towards anyone who desires to see women actually take ownership of themselves and act like adults, rather than pigs in heat. Since most women choose emotionalism before logic, we are unlikely to see any firm change in the future.

What makes the victim-blaming complex ridiculous is how feminists are themselves guilty of the same crime depending on who they specifically intend to target. When it comes to any minority group viewed as being the subject of persecution by white males, feminists will reliably change their tune. A wonderful example to show this is enshrined in Henriette Reker, the Mayor of Cologne. Reker rose to power as a herald for mainstream progressives with the support of numerous liberal and centrist groups. A major aspect in her platform was the assumption to stand in favor immigration on the part of the thousands of Arabs and Africans streaming into Europe by boat and on foot. On New Year's Eve in 2015, hundreds of women reported being sexually assaulted by these same parasites from the African continent. Reker's response was to adopt the very same tactics abhorred by progressive feminists in Western societies. Her statement to a reporter was as follows: "There's always the possibility of keeping a certain distance of more than a arm's length-that is to say make sure yourself you don't look to be too close to people who are not known to you, and to whom you don't have a trusting relationship."[61] In plainer words, victim blaming. In this instance it is fine, as women enmeshed with the feminist movement have a really pitiful obsession with white males as animals, but see black and Arab who rape as individuals expressing their diverse culture. They will stereotype white men in the least flattering light ala Brock Allen Turner, only to turn over (and undress) for males with a more diverse appearance, because those lads cannot commit sexual assault.

Adding to such insanity, feminist activist Steven Singer wrote the article "I'm a Public School Teacher—Give Me All the Refugees You've Got!" The piece employs quite bland prose meant to pull heartstrings about Arab refugees and emotions. After some needed allusions to white privilege and social status he gargles the following: "It is my responsibility to offer a helping hand in every way I can to those on the lower rungs. It is my joy to be able to see it."[62] For starters, we have already covered the worthless degeneracy that is the public school system, and its failure to produce good students. On top of that, Singer's pro-refugee stance should come as no surprise, as his professional field is

---

[61] Satlin, A. (2016, January 07). German Mayor Says Women Should Stand Away From Strangers To Avoid Being Attacked. *The Huffington Post*. Retrieved from http://www.huffingtonpost.com/entry/henriette-reker-cologne-attacks_us_568e3723e4b0c8beacf5c164
[62] Singer, S. (2015, December 26). I'm a Public School Teacher – Give Me All the Refugees You've Got! [Web log post]. Retrieved from http://everydayfeminism.com/2015/12/public-school-teacher-refugees/

jam-packed with folks who suck taxpayer money from the direct debit dole whilst churning out more dependents for the world to take care of. Teachers are hardly affected by the presence of refugees in the system, as they rely on government paychecks which are guaranteed regardless of the crime being foisted on women as a direct result of savages being dumped into Western countries. Singer will also get his pension one day, because as leftists and feminists believe, lazy refugees are actually hard workers who will pay taxes to fund those retirement plans.

Feminism has even gone far enough in its pollution of the mind to where individuals who have been sexually assaulted are excusing the behavior of their attackers. In 2010 progressive activist Amanda Kijera traveled to Haiti as part of a humanitarian mission to restore the country after it fell to the earthquake of 2009. Part of Kijera's activism entailed writing about the way women are treated in the island country and advocating against violence, both noble causes draped with the veil of tolerance. One night after her normal routine at work she was accosted and raped by a Haitian man. She describes the horrific ordeal:

> I begged him to stop. Afraid he would kill me, I pleaded with him to honor my commitment to Haiti, to him as a brother in the mutual struggle for an end to our common oppression, but to no avail. He didn't care that I was a Malcolm X scholar. He told me to shut up, and then slapped me in the face....Not once did I envision myself becoming a receptacle for a Black man's rage at the white world, but that is what I became. While I take issue with my brother's behavior, I'm grateful for the experience.[63]

---

[63] Goad, J. (2016, April 11). Grab Your Ankles and Let Them In. Taki's Mag. Retrieved from
http://takimag.com/article/grab_your_ankles_and_let_them_in_jim_goad/print#axzz4Wub
Yykma

The fact that she would revert to appealing to her work as a reason for him to stop the assault is disturbing enough, because it suggests there are legitimate grounds for other women to be raped. More bizarre would be her approach in the aftermath of the event. Rather than rejecting the violent and criminal nature of her attacker she attempted to defend his actions by BLAMING WHITE MEN. She said: "Black men have every right to the anger they feel in response to their position in the global hierarchy, but their anger is misdirected."[64]

Kijera goes on to blame colonialism for oppressing black people, in her own way justifying the actions of the man who sexually assaulted her. What's most peculiar is that Haiti was a slave colony until it overthrew European leadership in the 1800s, and has since been under the domination of blacks. The poor performance of Haiti as a country is not due to whites, as over 5,000 were slaughtered during the uprising , and the existing population there is quite miniscule.

Here we should perhaps engage in some meditation to comprehend the livid separation between normal cancer and the feminist equivalent. Typically individuals stricken with any variations of the disease are blatantly aware and try to keep in high spirits as they undergo the struggle of treatment. From these stories was birthed the concept of "fighting" cancer, with courageous patients refusing any manner of concession to the plague. The population spans young children and the elderly, as well as everyone in between, each committed to resist the destructive objectives of the sickness.

Our feminist associates are rather different. People such as the Haitian humanitarian worker are more than happy with their affliction; instead of pursuing a cure they greedily consume anything that will bring cancer closer to fruition, allowing its pink

---

[64] Cassiel, A. (2016, July 07). Diversity and the Rape of Justice. Retrieved from http://www.counter-currents.com/2016/07/diversity-and-the-rape-of-justice/

mass to change and dement their minds. Only from this can they manage to harvest the mentality sown before. Violent crimes may be excused as long as the perpetrator is not white, entire lives destroyed or violated; still the march goes on, supporting the contorted feminist definition of equality.

17. Destruction of Women

At this point we need to discuss how cancerous feminism is being employed as a fig leaf to ruin the lives of women by causing them to reject their natural roles. If a female dresses well or learns to cook, feminists immediately shriek that she is supporting outdated conceptions of gender. Settling down to raise children, arguably the most important job in society, smells strongly of traitorism as a result of the same poisons which hold women back in the world. Even the slightest adherence to traditional ideas of the family results in endless shaming from various components of the elite political and social class. The feminist view holds that women should pursue their own interests ahead of children, the one aspect guaranteed to bring out their most fundamental biological drives to care for and to love. Some rancid hot pockets have gone so far as to say women ought to abandon men altogether and embrace lesbianism, relying on submissive men only for the needed donation which can allow their sex-selective abortions to go on until synthetic alternatives can be found for the pastry bag injector.

All these choices may fit the mental illness often passing as keen feminist logic, but it holds grim tidings for the future. Already women outnumber men substantially in the West and have been forced to go abroad to find alternatives in a market where males have an incentive to delay marriage and enjoy diverse options. Why might they take this path as opposed to lesbianism? Simply put, being lesbian is a short-term phase that women grow out of once they begin to realize they are getting older and need a child to provide their life with meaning. A lesbian will never be happy because she is fighting her basic instinct to be taken and impregnated by a man. As we already know, in the Animal Kingdom securing strong male mates is imperative to the survival of the female on the planet. Sperm donations in contrast will come from weak and dithering parasites looking to make a quick buck off the desperate and bull dyke-esque. Even if she manages to secure decent spermatozoa it will come far removed from the strength and intimidation native to a real man while he conquers her emotionally and physically.

One cannot afford to overlook the weight of female sexuality on this equation. Any woman who rejects traditional sexual relations for a prostituted equivalent like carpet-munching will soon find herself driven insane by her inability to fulfill what nature intended. All women desire at the deepest level to be submissive to a man and have his children. This fact is supported by thousands of years of recorded history and the practical knowledge that women love being taken from behind while a man slaps their bottom. Feminists know this too, yet they invent fake ideas to hide their dirtiest needs from the curious eyes of the public square.

The long-term effect of the feminist project will be as follows: the sluts continue their quest for liberation, while the lesbian ranks slowly swell. Men refuse to marry these women, and either remain single or seek brides abroad. Those who choose to marry sluts soon divorce, because studies show women who have had many sexual partners are plagued with unhappiness and depression in their marriages.[65] Miserable women proceed to drink cheap wine and eat buckets of Crisco-lathered Wonder Bread, causing obesity in America to balloon, and leading to more heart disease and lesbians. An occasional illegal immigrant

---

[65] Tillin, T. (2014, August 24). New Study Claims People Who've Had More Sexual Partners Report Unhappier Marriages. *The Huffington Post*. Retrieved from http://www.huffingtonpost.com/2014/08/21/more-sexual-partners-unhappy-marriage_n_5698440.html

from Guatemala claims a fat American wife in order to get papers. Their relationship stays within the realm of oral sex because he might otherwise be crushed if she chose to ride.

Due to the lack of men marrying, feminists lobby governments for new public welfare programs to support women who do not feel like working. Bitter and crusty women stare in envy over their four fat positive chins at the gorgeous and fit women from foreign countries walking arm-in-arm with the men they seem unable to attain. The sport of hog-hunting becomes popular with teenage boys; they head out on the weekend and place bets on who can "ride the wave" and conquer a fat chick first.

Or there is another possibility. The entire feminist project collapses, leaving disaster in the wake. I for one suspect this to be inevitable, as the regularly-practiced antics of the feminist brand lead invariably towards cognitive dissonance and a drop in relevance for its followers. No one will happily join a movement that gets such terrible press, at least not in the record numbers needed to ensure its fledgling nature is not battered helpless against the winds of irrelevance and depravity.

Ultimately the way to rationalize the behavior of women who rise up and become violent fanatics in service the empty cause is by looking at their own backgrounds. It is rare to find a feminist, for instance, who does not have foundations in a broken household or experience with sexual molestation. Famed feminist attention-grabber Lena Dunham is a fine example to match this reality. She is renown, for among other things, making rape accusations against someone part of the College Republicans at Oberlin College. Substantial media investigations suggested she had lied, and falsely accused one man in particular of the act.[66] The truly juicy revelation came when Dunham wrote in lurid detail

---

[66] Collman, A., Nathan, S., McCormack, D., & De Graaf, M. (2014, December 09). Lena Dunham breaks silence to say she gave her rapist a pseudonym to protect HIM as she apologizes to man falsely identified as her attacker Read more: http://www.dailymail.co.uk/news/article-2867898/Lena-Dunham-breaks-silence-say-gave-

about sexually exploring her younger sister when she was a teenager, including "finding" pebbles in the child's vagina.[67] To feminists this sort of behavior can be passed off as the result of "courage "and "strength" against the common mores of society. Of course things are far simpler. All decent human beings know molesting a child is wrong, and false accusations that shred a target's reputation deserve harsh repercussions under the law. Only in the warped and corroded mind of a feminist can these things be described as inspirational.

More than anything else, feminism springs from a desperate desire to express anger at the world for any number of issues which normal folks can resolve without reaching for the toxic discus of the pink flamingo. Often times it is the result of poor looks and a lack of attention from the opposite sex. A girl might be grossly obese or lack fashion sense in contrast to her fitter and classier peers. Rather than turning this into a cause for self-improvement, she launches a Tumblr blog and rages about the need for fat positivity in order to smash Patriarchy. Still no one will have sex with her, so she adopts fat positive lesbianism and continues to grow angrier by the passing day, taking every opportunity to beat down and shame decent women who embody femininity and seek after happiness with men.

The other possibility is poor relationships with her parents. Maybe her father was distant, if not a flaming homosexual. Instead of trying to find a better man who might boost her own chances at having a good life and raising children, she swears off both in favor the savory indulgence of multiple men while at the same time doing social work to promote

---

rapist-pseudonym-protect-apologizes-man-falsely-identified-
attacker.html#ixzz4XqGMQ1Bw Retrieved from http://www.dailymail.co.uk/news/article-2867898/Lena-Dunham-breaks-silence-say-gave-rapist-pseudonym-protect-apologizes-man-falsely-identified-attacker.html

[67] Flood, A. (2014, November 05). Lena Dunham apologises after critics accuse her of sexually molesting sister. *The Guardian*. Retrieved from https://www.theguardian.com/books/2014/nov/05/lena-dunham-statement-abuse-claims

female dignity. Her demeanor, once destined to be pleasant and sweetened, is caught in a brittle, cobweb-coated chamber pot of feminism, where it is capable of exhibiting only violent hatred.

With the entire glassy image of feminism in view, the question survives as to what can be done about it. Cancer normally can be treated through a combination of chemotherapy and radiation, surgery, or other procedures, the goal being to neutralize the growth so it cannot spread and further infect the body. While the survival rate has not yet reached 100 percent, improvements in technology and medicine have made the various treatment methods more likely to bring about positive results than seen in previous years. Ideally, chemotherapy will reach a point when it can be targeted to avoid collateral damage which threatens other critical life support systems.

In the case of the feminist cancer, the disease has so ravaged society that it must be cut out through a long and coordinated process beginning with mindset. Anyone who is under the spell of the sickness must be slowly and carefully coaxed towards taking the Red Pill, so they awaken to all the destruction caused by the Excited Estrogen Club. The most advanced stage of this problem is typified in the unhinged Tumblr blogs calling for men to be destroyed and urging womenfolk in the direction of Lesbos. Creatures sworn to the negative mentality must be cowed, or at the very least deported to places where they can do no harm to Western Civilization, such as North Korea. Our biggest advantage in this regard lies with the follower nature of women. If the herd begins to pursue new directions, women will fall in line without questions because they ae at the scintillating level submissive things who treasure the guidance of strong men. It is primarily due to the feckless and frequently homosexual behavior exhibited by men that ladies have turned to fill the void of masculinity. We can change the trajectory by helping men act like they were built to be and reinforcing positive role models for girls. For the record, Lena Dunham, Hillary Clinton, and Margaret Cho are all horrible examples.

We can begin the process of cleansing by training boys to be men, not skirt-flashing nightclub attendees who fellate manly women out by the dumpster. From a young age boys need to be taught they are different than girls and shown that their place is to be complimented, and not equaled, by females. All co-ed sports ought to be banned for this reason, and boys allowed to pursue physical activities that make them men, like boxing and rifle shooting clubs. The latter were immensely popular in American public schools until women and a broader collective of mixed gender morons took over the educational administration. Young men also need opportunities to strike out sooner in life. Keeping a boy cooped up in a government classroom past the age of fourteen so he can listen to some crone shot up on Xanax talk about the Wage Gap is insanity. He should be free to work, learn a trade, or run a business instead; all of these things have stronger bearings on his ability to succeed than "Social Studies" and "Physical Education." Mixing boys with boys will inevitably marshal better social skills and respect for authority than is seen in schools, where petty gossip and sophomoric systems of popularity still predominate.

When it comes to girls, they should be taught to dress in ways that heighten their femininity instead of projecting lesbianism, or showcasing the jewels from Whore Island. They should learn to darn, cook, sing, and make music, all skills lost to the population of Starbucks lovers and insane suffragette upstarts. Education should emphasize classics like *Pride and Prejudice*, and not mutilated perversions like the multitude of sexual bondage novels passed off as high caliber by the snot-gargling oafs of modern institutions.

In regards to interaction between the sexes, they would be best centered on events signaling the normal decency of couples. Local dances and talent shows are possibilities, and certainly far superior to the drug and alcohol-fueled hookups which dominate college campuses and leave females struggling to form emotional bonds in life. Concurrently, girls ought to be raised valuing their sexual purity and compelled to find a good man in their early twenties at the latest, rather than waiting ten years while sampling the varying offers of disease-carrying appendages in a mad quest to attain personal validation.

The matter must extend of course to the family. Fathers are the first line of defense when it comes to the healthy maturation of their daughters, and should be good role models. If they take the limp-dicked approach of a cuckhold and refuse to rein in the young machinations of women, they are contributing to the problem. Before leading their daughters they have to dominate their wives sexually, financially, and through a strong personality. This starts by not wedding expired old prostitutes out of desperation, because such specimens will make poor examples for their children. The mere idea passed on by some mothers to their daughters encouraging "experimentation" before marriage is heinous and should be responded by a fierce tongue-lashing at minimum. At the very base it explains why girls choose the mantle of whoredom early in their lives, while the mass media is also greatly to blame.

On the same note, the media should be reformed to reflect ideal examples for girls to follow. Rather than the Kim Kardashians and Chelsea Handlers that prepopulate every channel, encouraging prostitution as the highest calling, young women ought to see some of the best and brightest of their sex, individuals who strive to be good mothers, teachers, and wives. Any producer who endorses ramshackle morals and the portrayal of women as free spirited usb ports must be arrested and fined heavily to protect the interests of society. If there is no market of value for sleaze, it will stop being produced.

To promote healthy lifestyles amongst young women, we must introduce a broader culture of fat-shaming. Most tropical countries already have such concepts ingrained out of necessity because of the temperature and beach life, but in the marginally colder north women appear to think storing extra cottage cheese in their thighs, stomach, and behind will endear them to the mutated zombie wolves once civilization collapses. No doubt they are correct, but only with a side of ketchup.

The specific advantage contained in a fat-negative environment is the potential for massive heath improvements. A skinnier population means less fat-related medical conditions driving up the cost of the "free" healthcare feminists so desperately want. We would also save millions of gallons of fuel each year that is currently employed to carry the added weight supplied by our bull dyke sisters. And there is of course the heavy consumption of food, which is bound to drop like a rock once women adjust to eating according to needed nutrition rather than going by their nerves or gluttony. As we noted before, the collectivist mentality carried by women in general suggests they will begin to converge rapidly once this behavior is adopted by the mainstream. Women do not enjoy being the odd (read: unattractive) one out, thus their cooperation should be expected.

In the economic realm, the government should immediately cease all payments of alimony and subsidies for birth control, as well as public housing. All these programs along with food stamps are overwhelmingly utilized by women to fatten themselves at the taxpayer's expense. Millions of men and a handful of responsible women work hard each and every day to prop up moronic single mothers whose greatest claim to fame is the supposedly "heroic" act of not remembering to take the birth control pill one or twice. They will spend months and years living on the role, pumping out low IQ brats who stand little chance of succeeding beyond what their wench of an afterthought mother amounted to. If women no longer have a financial incentive, they will close their legs and look for decent men to bed down with instead of the flotsam of the world.

Obviously this segment is not complete by discussing how the juvenile nature of women can be corrected through some common sense. We have long since established that females are highly emotional children incapable of functioning without strict oversight. Their entire existence revolves around feelings and impulse-driven desires. Remove both these elements as primary aspects and you get the slumbering movement towards decency that the world needs.

As an addendum, women should not be permitted to vote. Since they typically take out more than they contribute, it is not just that they have the same political stake in the system used to levy taxes on actual worker bees. The enfranchisement of women only heightened the national decline by allowing emotion-based ballots to flood elections and bring aboard left-wing cockroaches such as Barack Obama, who is himself the product of a single mother who could not keep her skirt on. Women fail to use any logic or quantitative reasoning when selecting candidates, as evidenced by the luxurious stream of issues even today which are labeled as "women's" and used to create monolith voting blocs for the most liberal candidates.

By preventing women from voting we will create a new meritocracy to ensure ladies take into account real financial issues when they go about tossing their ballots down the long, computerized shoot. No more will airheaded feminists be able to latch birth control or meaningless complaints about misogyny onto their choices in elections at any level. Behind their capricious aspirations will be a man, ready and strong of opinion to moderate the flair of her mental instability.

Finally, women will ideally be shooed out of the workforce and back to their rightful place as mothers and homemakers. The corrupt feminist experiment of liberation through cancerous infection has not made women freer; instead they are more easily angered, age quicker, and develop mental illness in record numbers. Stressful demands of careers versus children have turned a generation into flagrant whores who suck dick in their twenties and kiss children in their thirties. We cannot allow the status quo to continue unhindered. Women must be recused from themselves. The cancer that is ravaging them needs treatment. Feminism must face the sane judgment of the world to save women and the planet as a whole.

The End

References

Antle, W. (2009, December 4). *Democrat Wars. The American Spectator. Retrieved from https://spectator.org/40441_democrat-wars/*

ATTN: Women shouldn't have to spend a fortune on bras. [Video file]. (2016, July 1). Retrieved from https://www.facebook.com/attn/videos/1082052741830184/

Baker, J. (2014, August 17). 6 Things That I Understand About the Fat-Acceptance Movement. Retrieved from http://everydayfeminism.com/2014/08/i-understand-fat-acceptance-movement/

Ball, J. (2013, May 23). Women 40% more likely than men to develop mental illness, study finds. *The Guardian.* Retrieved from https://www.theguardian.com/society/2013/may/22/women-men-mental-illness-study

BDSM And Feminism: "Stop Telling Me What I'm Supposed To Like, D*mn It." [Web log interview]. (2010, October 17). Retrieved from http://jezebel.com/5666107/bdsm-and-feminism-stop-telling-me-what-im-supposed-to-like-dmn-it

Bellstrom, K. (2015, December 10). Elizabeth Holmes Hints at Sexism in Media Coverage. *Fortune.* Retrieved from http://fortune.com/2015/12/10/elizabeth-holmes-sexism-theranos/

Bloomfield, J. (2015, February 18). 5 Reasons Women Love Rape Fantasies. *Thought Catalog.* Retrieved from http://thoughtcatalog.com/janet-bloomfield/2015/02/5-reasons-women-love-rape-fantasies/

Bloomfield, J. (2016, August 16). Reblog: Research find that as a group, only men pay tax [Web log post]. Retrieved from http://judgybitch.com/2016/08/16/reblog-research-find-that-as-a-group-only-men-pay-tax/

Breslin, S. (2011, August 4). Why Men Are Better Negotiators Than Women. *Forbes*. Retrieved from http://www.forbes.com/sites/susannahbreslin/2011/08/04/why-men-are-better-negotiators-than-women/#3c1476fe3fcd

Brown, Elizabeth. "The 'Pink Tax' Is a Myth." *Reason.com*. N.p., 05 Jan. 2016. Web. Retrieved from http://reason.com/blog/2016/01/05/the-pink-tax-is-a-myth

Bruner, R. (2016, October 12). This Pharmacy Instituted a Controversial 7% 'Man Tax' to Call Out Price Discrimination [Web log post]. Retrieved from http://time.com/4528451/pharmacy-man-tax/

Burton, C. (2015, September 25). COVER STORY: NEW LINES. GQ UK. Retrieved from http://www.gq-magazine.co.uk/article/emily-ratajkowski-we-are-your-friends-blurred-lines

Bussel, R. (2016, April 16). Right-wing trolls attack #ShoutYourStatus campaign: "American feminists now feel the need to brag about what stds they've caught". *Salon*. Retrieved from http://www.salon.com/2016/04/14/rightwing_trolls_attack_shoutyourstatus_campaign_american_feminists_now_feel_the_need_to_brag_about_what_stds_theyve_caught/

Carlson, K. J., Eisenstat, S. A., & Ziporyn, T. D. (2004). *The new Harvard guide to women's health*. Cambridge, MA: Harvard University Press.

Cassiel, A. (2016, July 07). Diversity and the Rape of Justice. Retrieved from http://www.counter-currents.com/2016/07/diversity-and-the-rape-of-justice/

Collman, A., Nathan, S., McCormack, D., & De Graaf, M. (2014, December 09). Lena Dunham breaks silence to say she gave her rapist a pseudonym to protect HIM as she apologizes to man falsely identified as her attacker Read more: http://www.dailymail.co.uk/news/article-2867898/Lena-Dunham-breaks-silence-say-gave-rapist-pseudonym-protect-apologizes-man-falsely-identified-attacker.html#ixzz4XqGMQ1Bw

Collins, D. (2004, November 05). U.S.: Fat Fliers Swell Fuel Costs. Retrieved from http://www.cbsnews.com/news/us-fat-fliers-swell-fuel-costs/

Council for American Private Education. (n.d.). Retrieved from http://www.capenet.org/facts.html

Crocker, L. (2015, September 21). Why the New 'One in Four' Campus Rape Statistic Is Misleading. *The Daily Beast*. Retrieved from http://www.thedailybeast.com/articles/2015/09/21/how-misleading-is-the-new-one-in-four-campus-rape-statistic.html

Davies, M. (2015, September 28). 'I'm 27 stone but have NO desire to be thin': Fat Girl Dancing and TV star Whitney Thore speaks out about her battle with polycystic ovaries – and why the link between obesity and health problems is exaggerated Retrieved from http://www.dailymail.co.uk/health/article-3247597/I-m-27-stone-NO-desire-Fat-Girl-Dancing-TV-star-Whitney-Thore-speaks-battle-polycystic-ovaries-link-obesity-health-problems-exaggerated.html#ixzz4WdlFKiDI .

Durando, J. (2015, November 05). Canadian PM Justin Trudeau says cabinet is half women 'because it's 2015' USA TODAY. Retrieved from http://www.usatoday.com/story/news/nation-now/2015/11/05/prime-minister-canada-women-cabinet-justin-trudeau/75207820/

Dvorak, P. (2015, July 23). Frigid offices, freezing women, oblivious men: An air-conditioning investigation. *The Washington Post*. Retrieved from http://www.highbeam.com/doc/1P2-38549984.html?refid=easy_hf

Evon, D. (2015, December 30). Hillary Clinton and the Victims of War. Retrieved from http://www.snopes.com/hillary-clinton-victims-of-war/

Fairchild, C. (2012, October 09). Gas Mileage, Costs Affected By Driver's Weight. Retrieved from http://www.huffingtonpost.com/2012/10/09/gas-mileage-costs-affected-by-drivers-weight_n_1951174.html

Fast Facts. (n.d.). Retrieved from https://nces.ed.gov/fastfacts/display.asp?id=28

Feminist own goal [Web log post]. (2016, March 17). Retrieved from http://didactsreach.blogspot.com/2016/03/feminist-own-goal.html

Fiano, C. (2009, December 18). Feminist: Husbands and fathers are "useless hunks of flesh" [Web log post]. Retrieved from http://hotair.com/greenroom/archives/2009/12/18/feminist-husbands-and-fathers-are-useless-hunks-of-flesh/

Filipovic, J. (2006, June 19). Feminist Politics of Blowjob [Web log post]. Retrieved from http://www.feministe.us/blog/archives/2006/06/19/feminist-politics-of-blowjobs/

Flood, A. (2014, November 05). Lena Dunham apologises after critics accuse her of sexually molesting sister. *The Guardian*. Retrieved from https://www.theguardian.com/books/2014/nov/05/lena-dunham-statement-abuse-claims

Forney, M. (April 26). Student Accused Of Rape By Emma Sulkowicz To Sue Columbia University [Web log post]. Retrieved from http://www.returnofkings.com/62253/student-accused-of-rape-by-emma-sulkowicz-to-sue-columbia-university

Freeman, A. (2015, August 18). Single Moms and Welfare Woes: A Higher-Education Dilemma. *The Atlantic*. Retrieved from https://www.theatlantic.com/education/archive/2015/08/why-single-moms-struggle-with-college/401582/

Gandhi, K. (2015, April 26). Sisterhood, blood and boobs at the London Marathon 2015 [Web log post]. Retrieved from https://madamegandhi.blog/2015/04/26/sisterhood-blood-and-boobs-at-the-london-marathon-2015/

George, K. (2014, November 19). Femen Protestors Shove Crucifixes Up Their Bums In Vatican Square — VIDEO [Web log post]. Retrieved from https://www.bustle.com/articles/49905-femen-protestors-shove-crucifixes-up-their-bums-in-vatican-square-video

Goad, J. (2016, April 11). Grab Your Ankles and Let Them In. *Taki's Mag*. Retrieved from http://takimag.com/article/grab_your_ankles_and_let_them_in_jim_goad/print#axzz4Wub Yykma

Goldenberg, A. R. (2016, June 28). NOW Calls Girl Who Falsely Cried Rape an 'Inspiration' to Real Rape Victims [Web log post]. Retrieved from http://www.mrctv.org/blog/now-calls-girl-who-famously-cried-rape-inspiration-real-rape-victims

Greenfield, D. (2016, May 03). WHY WON'T ANYONE TALK ABOUT WHAT A TERRIBLE CEO MARISSA MAYER IS? Front Page Mag. Retrieved from http://www.frontpagemag.com/point/262704/why-wont-anyone-talk-about-what-terrible-ceo-daniel-greenfield

Groom, N. (2017, January 24). 'What a disaster': Top scientist says high school physics is being 'feminised' - with difficult equations taken out of exams to make the subject more appealing to girls. *Daily Mail*. Retrieved from http://www.dailymail.co.uk/news/article-4151966/Michelle-Simmons-says-HSC-curriculum-changes-horriying.html#ixzz4YEAD4nBF

Harrington, C. (2016, March 29). There's a Reason It's Hard to Find Cheap Bras. *Teen Vogue*. Retrieved from http://www.teenvogue.com/story/cost-of-lingerie-explainer

Hawks, A. (2015, May 16). Whitney Thore explains how feminism and fat positivity are connected [Web log post]. Retrieved from http://starcasm.net/archives/315776

Johnson, C. (2016, November 04). #RollingStoneTrial: GotNews & Chuck Johnson Bring Down Rolling Stone Over #JackieCoakley. Retrieved from http://gotnews.com/rollingstonetrial-gotnews-chuck-johnson-bring-rolling-stone-jackiecoakley/

Knapton, S. (2014, October 01). Could previous lovers influence appearance of future children? The Telegraph. Retrieved from http://www.telegraph.co.uk/news/science/science-news/11133203/Could-previous-lovers-influence-appearance-of-future-children.html

Lodi, M. (2015, July 23). Is Office Air Conditioning a Sexist Conspiracy? Jezebel. Retrieved from http://jezebel.com/is-office-air-conditioning-a-sexist-conspiracy-1719883384

Mack, L. (2016, August 17). 7 Ways Doggy Style is Actually a Feminist Choice [Web log post]. Retrieved from https://www.romper.com/p/7-ways-doggy-style-is-actually-a-feminist-choice-16519

Marusic, K. (2015, September 08). This Twenty-Something Got Herpes, And Now She's On A Mission To Tell Everyone About It. Retrieved from http://www.mtv.com/news/2264301/ella-dawson-herpes-on-a-mission-to-tell-everyone/

Mazziotta, J. (2016, May 5). My Big Fat Fabulous Life: Whitney Way Thore Rushed to the Hospital for Exhaustion. *People*. Retrieved from http://people.com/tv/whitney-way-thore-my-big-fat-fabulous-life-star-rushed-to-hospital/

Mazziotta, J. (2015, June 15). WATCH: Whitney Way Thore Gets a Wake-Up Call at the Hospital – 'I Need to Have Healthy Habits' *People*. Retrieved from http://people.com/bodies/whitney-way-thore-gets-a-wake-up-call-at-the-hospital/

McGregor, J. (2016, July 18). As Yahoo sale nears, do women in tech get pushed more onto the 'glass cliff'? *The Washington Post*. Retrieved from https://www.washingtonpost.com/news/on-leadership/wp/2016/07/18/as-yahoo-sale-nears-do-women-in-tech-get-pushed-more-onto-the-glass-cliff/?utm_term=.42d600ae9b3e

Motion picture on Television Program. (2013). Australia: InsightSBS. Retrieved from https://www.youtube.com/watch?v=v6mMpE8AaA0

Pearson, C. (2015, May 05). 14 Men and Women Get Very, Very Real About Period Sex [Web log post]. Retrieved from http://www.huffingtonpost.com/entry/14-men-and-women-get-very-very-real-about-period-sex_us_572cb40ee4b016f378957b12

Russian punks "Pussy Riot" and chicken in the vagina! . (2012, July 23). Retrieved from http://www.liveleak.com/view?i=aea_1343072683

Sanghani, R. (2015, July 24). Air conditioning in your office is sexist. True story. *The Telegraph*. Retrieved from http://www.telegraph.co.uk/women/womens-life/11760417/Air-conditioning-in-your-office-is-sexist.-True-story.html

Satlin, A. (2016, January 07). German Mayor Says Women Should Stand Away From Strangers To Avoid Being Attacked. *The Huffington Post*. Retrieved from http://www.huffingtonpost.com/entry/henriette-reker-cologne-attacks_us_568e3723e4b0c8beacf5c164

Singer, S. (2015, December 26). I'm a Public School Teacher – Give Me All the Refugees You've Got! [Web log post]. Retrieved from http://everydayfeminism.com/2015/12/public-school-teacher-refugees/

United States, Department of Labor, Bureau of Labor Statistics. (2008). *Quick Facts on Registered Nurses (RNs)*. Retrieved from https://www.dol.gov/wb/factsheets/Qf-nursing-08.htm

United States, Internal Revenue Service, Statistics of Income Division. (2012). *Data on Salaries and Wages and Business Income, by Gender, Tax Year 2009*. Retrieved from https://www.irs.gov/pub/irs-soi/09in01gender.pdf

Thompson, D. (2012, December 18). 7 Facts About Government Benefits and Who Gets Them. *The Atlantic*.

Tillin, T. (2014, August 24). New Study Claims People Who've Had More Sexual Partners Report Unhappier Marriages. *The Huffington Post*. Retrieved from http://www.huffingtonpost.com/2014/08/21/more-sexual-partners-unhappy-marriage_n_5698440.html

Tobak, S. (2011, March 08). The Gender Pay Gap is a Complete Myth. Retrieved from http://www.cbsnews.com/news/the-gender-pay-gap-is-a-complete-myth/

Tran, R. (2016, June 19). 4 Ways Men Are Taught to Objectify Women From Birth [Web log post]. Retrieved from http://everydayfeminism.com/2016/06/men-taught-to-objectify-women/

Valenti, J. (2015, July 17). Ellen Pao isn't harassed because she's female. It's because she's a feminist. *The Guardian*. Retrieved from https://www.theguardian.com/commentisfree/2015/jul/17/ellen-pao-harassment-feminist

Wakeman, J. (2010, March 02). Girl Talk: I Wanted To Be Dominated [Web log post]. Retrieved from http://www.thefrisky.com/2010-03-02/girl-talk-i-wanted-to-be-dominated/

What Are the Health Risks of Overweight and Obesity? (2012, July 13). Retrieved from https://www.nhlbi.nih.gov/health/health-topics/topics/obe/risks

Women Re-Create The Victoria Secret Fashion Show. (2016, December 08). Retrieved from https://www.youtube.com/watch?v=45V61KHcr2E

About the Author

Thomas Rogers is a brilliant philosopher and lover of women from the Deep South. He spent several years in the tumultuous hell of the labor market before becoming a full-time business owner and writer. Apart from resisting the skullduggery of the modern world, he enjoys traveling, gardening, and the occasional bottle of Jack Daniels.